Best Outdoor Adventures Near
PORTLAND, OREGON

A Guide to the City's Greatest
Hiking, Paddling, and Cycling

ADAM SAWYER

FALCONGUIDES

GUILFORD, CONNECTICUT
HELENA, MONTANA

FALCONGUIDES®

An imprint of Rowman & Littlefield
Falcon, FalconGuides, and Chockstone are registered trademarks and Make Adventure Your Story is a trademark of Rowman & Littlefield.

Distributed by NATIONAL BOOK NETWORK

Copyright © 2016 Rowman & Littlefield
Maps: Melissa Baker © Rowman & Littlefield
Photos by Adam Sawyer

British Library Cataloguing-in-Publication Information available

Library of Congress Cataloging-in-Publication Data

Names: Sawyer, Adam, 1974- author.
Title: Best outdoor adventures near Portland, Oregon : a guide to the city's greatest hiking, paddling, and cycling / Adam Sawyer.
Description: Guilford, Connecticut : FalconGuides, [2016] | Includes index. | "Distributed by National Book Network"—T.p. verso.
Identifiers: LCCN 2016016995 (print) | LCCN 2016018195 (ebook) | ISBN 9781493017102 (pbk. : alk. paper) | ISBN 9781493017119 (e-book)
Subjects: LCSH: Outdoor recreation—Oregon—Portland Region—Guidebooks. | Portland Region (Or.)—Guidebooks.
Classification: LCC GV191.42.O7 S28 2016 (print) | LCC GV191.42.O7 (ebook) | DDC 796.509795/49—dc23
LC record available at https://lccn.loc.gov/2016016995

∞™ The paper used in this publication meets the minimum requirements of American National Standard for Information Sciences—Permanence of Paper for Printed Library Materials, ANSI/NISO Z39.48-1992.

The author and Rowman & Littlefield assume no liability for accidents happening to, or injuries sustained by, readers who engage in the activities described in this book.

Contents

Overview

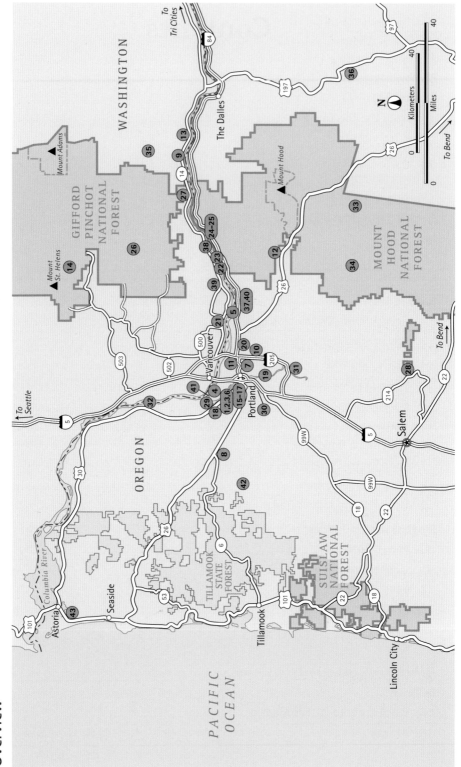

Help Us Keep This Guide Up to Date

Every effort has been made by the author and editors to make this guide as accurate and useful as possible. However, many things can change after a guide is published—trails and routes are modified, water flow fluctuates, regulations change, facilities come under new management, and so forth.

We welcome your comments concerning your experiences with this guide and how you feel it could be improved and kept up to date. While we may not be able to respond to all comments and suggestions, we'll take them to heart, and we'll also make certain to share them with the author. Please send your comments and suggestions to the following address:

FalconGuides
Reader Response/Editorial Department
246 Goose Lane
Guilford, CT 06437

Or you may e-mail us at:

editorial@falcon.com

Thanks for your input, and enjoy!

WARNING:

CLIMBING IS A SPORT WHERE YOU MAY BE SERIOUSLY INJURED OR DIE. READ THIS BEFORE YOU USE THIS BOOK.

The latter section of this guidebook—the section regarding rock climbing—is a compilation of unverified information gathered from many different sources. The author cannot assure the accuracy of any of the information in this book, including the topos and route descriptions, the difficulty ratings, and the protection ratings. These may be incorrect or misleading, and it is impossible for any one author to climb all the routes to confirm the information about each route. Also, ratings of climbing difficulty and danger are always subjective and depend on the physical characteristics (for example, height), experience, technical ability, confidence, and physical fitness of the climber who supplied the rating. Additionally, climbers who achieve first ascents sometimes underrate the difficulty or danger of the climbing route out of fear of being ridiculed if a climb is later downrated by subsequent ascents. Therefore, be warned that you must exercise your own judgment on where a climbing route goes, its difficulty, and your ability to safely protect yourself from the risks of rock climbing. These risks include falling due to technical difficulty or due to natural hazards such as holds breaking, falling rock, climbing equipment dropped by other climbers, hazards of weather and lightning, your own equipment failure, and failure or absence of fixed protection.

You should not depend on any information gleaned from this book for your personal safety; your safety depends on your own good judgment, based on experience and a realistic assessment of your climbing ability. If you have any doubt as to your ability to safely climb a route described in this book, do not attempt it.

The following are some ways to make your use of this book safer:

1. Consultation. You should consult with other climbers about the difficulty and danger of a particular climb prior to attempting it. Most local climbers are glad to give advice on routes in their area, and we suggest that you contact locals to confirm ratings and the safety of particular routes and to obtain firsthand information about a route chosen from this book.

2. Instruction. Most climbing areas have local climbing instructors and guides available. We recommend that you engage an instructor or guide to learn safety techniques and to become familiar with the routes and hazards of the areas described in this book. Even after you are proficient in climbing safely,

occasional use of a guide is a safe way to raise your climbing standard and learn advanced techniques.

3. Fixed Protection. Because of variances in the manner of placement, and weathering of fixed protection, all fixed protection should be considered suspect and should always be backed up by equipment that you place yourself. Never depend for your safety on a single piece of fixed protection; you never can tell whether it will hold weight, and in some cases fixed protection may have been removed or is now absent.

Be aware of the following specific potential hazards that could arise in using this book:

1. Incorrect Route Descriptions. If you climb a route and have a doubt as to where the route may go, do not continue unless you are sure you can go that way safely. Route descriptions and topos in this book may be inaccurate or misleading.

2. Incorrect Difficulty Rating. A route may be more difficult than the rating indicates. Do not be lulled into a false sense of security by the difficulty rating.

3. Incorrect Protection Rating. If you climb a route and are unable to arrange adequate protection from the risk of falling through the use of fixed pitons or bolts and by placing your own protection devices, do not assume that there is adequate protection available higher just because the route protection rating indicates the route is not an "X" or an "R" rating. Every route is potentially an "X" (a fall may be deadly) due to the inherent hazards of climbing—including, for example, failure or absence of fixed protection, your own equipment's failure, or improper use of climbing equipment.

THERE ARE NO WARRANTIES, WHETHER EXPRESS OR IMPLIED, THAT THIS GUIDEBOOK IS ACCURATE OR THAT THE INFORMATION CONTAINED IN IT IS RELIABLE. THERE ARE NO WARRANTIES OF FITNESS FOR A PARTICULAR PURPOSE OR THAT THIS GUIDE IS MERCHANTABLE. EVERY EFFORT WAS MADE TO ENSURE ACCURACY, HOWEVER, YOUR USE OF THIS BOOK INDICATES YOUR ASSUMPTION OF THE RISK THAT IT MAY CONTAIN ERRORS AND IS AN ACKNOWLEDGMENT OF YOUR OWN SOLE RESPONSIBILITY FOR YOUR CLIMBING SAFETY.

Acknowledgments

Authoring a guidebook is a ton of work. This is my third effort, and for some reason I'm still surprised at how much time and energy guidebooks require. For me, an undertaking of this magnitude requires a team. I am lucky enough to be surrounded by a group of people who directly and indirectly supported me and this endeavor every step of the way. It may sound like a cliché, but this thing quite literally could not have been pulled off without them. And they are:

Katie Benoit Cardoso and John Burbidge, my people with FalconGuides. Your faith and assistance have proven invaluable, and I am eternally indebted for the opportunity. I would also like to apologize for any heartburn/ulcers I may have caused by playing fast and loose with regards to deadlines. Thanks to Kassidy Anderson and her wonderful parents, Toni and Jesse, for their unwavering support. Thanks to Portland Walking Tours and Evergreen Escapes for providing me with another outlet for telling people about this amazing place we call home. And thanks to Heather Egizio for always being my on-call hiking buddy. Big thanks to KEEN Footwear for the inspiration, support, and gear that have been helping me find adventures around Oregon and beyond for the last several years.

Thanks to everyone in my family—Jade Sawyer Chase, Janaira Quigley, Bill Sawyer, Cindy Sawyer, Thea Sawyer, and Ruby Hair. What you wonderful people have done for me over the course of my life, let alone this last year, essentially elevates you to sainthood.

Special thanks go to a group of friends who helped me through some difficult personal times: Dan Wakefield, Rebekah Voie, Anna Haller, Abigail Entrican, Leann Craft, Staci Humphrey, and Marc Alan Jordan. Your love and support saved my life. I love you all.

Straddling the line between the last paragraph and this one is my girlfriend, Kara Close. Your love, support, and company on some wonderful adventures have been invaluable. You help give me focus and perspective. You make me laugh until I cry, make me look up new words, and are the ultimate trivia wing woman. I love you, lady. Go team sunhat!

I would be remiss without thanking the people responsible for what I get to do for a living, and help keep my head above water: Lucy Gibson, Allen Cox, Dave Peterson, Nan Devlin, and Kim Cooper Findling.

Thanks to Jeff Statt and his family for all the support, including the use of the family van! Thank you, Blair Hoff, for your support, friendship, and VW! Thanks to Katherine Hoppe for ruling with an iron fist! Actually, I should be thanking you more in the next book, but I'm doing it here too. Thanks to Oregonhikers .org, Tom Kloster, Zach Forsyth, Tim Burke, Melinda Muckenthaler, Aaron Young, Jeffery Abbott, Bryan Swan, and all the other boundary-less explorers I know, who are constantly providing inspiration.

Thanks to everyone who came out to see me talk about waterfalls at public libraries around the state. You confirmed that this is a thing I should be doing. I hope to see you all again when I'm giving slideshow presentations for this book.

Thanks to everyone else who has helped along the way. Too many to list here, but you know who you are, and so do I!

Lastly, enormous thanks to Stephanie Paris. You have been my primary adventure buddy over the course of the last three years, and this book, let alone my career, would not exist without you. Your love, support, and adventurous spirit allowed me to soar. Thanks for being who you are, and thanks for being my friend. This book is dedicated to you.

Memorial Park Library
Self Checkout
March,19,2019 19:04

39065145689863   4/9/2019
Best outdoor adventures near Portland,
Oregon : a guide to the city's greatest
hiking, paddling, and cycling

Total   1 item(s)

You have 0 item(s) ready for pickup

To check your card and renew items

go to www.calgarylibrary.ca

or call 403-262-2928

Introduction

Portland, Oregon, is a special place. One of the primary reasons many of us choose to hang our hats here is the seemingly limitless outdoor recreation options. If there's something you like to do outside, chances are good that you can find it within 2 hours of Portland. What do you like doing? What would you like to try? It's here—or near here. A quick rundown of things to do includes hiking, trail running, kayaking, whitewater rafting, standup paddleboarding, surfing, kite boarding, cycling, mountain biking, mountain climbing, rock climbing, skiing, snowboarding, snowshoeing, horseback riding, paragliding, skydiving, ziplining, disc golf . . . the list is extensive.

Any real estate agent will give you an earful about "location." Portland benefits greatly from its location in many ways, but with regards to outdoor endeavors, we're sitting in the catbird seat. From downtown Portland you can get to the Columbia River Gorge in 30 minutes, have Mount Hood in your face in 1 hour, dip your toes in the Pacific Ocean in 90 minutes, and take in a sunset from the high desert in 2 hours. And within that radius are more creeks, rivers, trails,

Portland is an outdoor city with facilities and views everywhere.

1

lakes, peaks, valleys, and protected wilderness areas than any of us could ever see in a lifetime or more.

Over the last year and a half, I got to go traipsing around the greater Portland area with my friends, experiencing the best outdoor activities the region has to offer. And now it all culminates in a guidebook that, for me, also serves as a journal of these incredible experiences. Some of the best adventures I've had in my life were had while "working" on this book. It is my sincere hope that it can provide you with comparable experiences. I also encourage you to keep going. This book, while chock-full of some of the best stuff around, is more or less an *amuse-bouche* for what's out there. Within 2 hours of Portland, an immeasurable amount of adventure awaits.

How to Use This Guide

Each adventure entry gives a rundown of the essential particulars: how long, what kind of path, elevation, best times to go, what to look for, etc. Turn-by-turn directions, GPS coordinates, occasionally flowery descriptions of why you should be doing this thing, and photos are provided for each outing as well. To the best of my ability, I have provided all the information I think you'll need to have a fantastic time on any of these adventures.

That being stated, some discussion of precautions is in order. Always check conditions before you go—weather conditions, road conditions, and the condition of your gear. Maybe even check in with your physical and mental status before attempting something that's going to require more effort and fortitude than you encounter on a daily basis. If you know something is going to push your limits or test your boundaries, give it the proper consideration and preparation it deserves. Going on an adventure that extends you beyond your comfort level can make memories that last a lifetime. It can also get you into trouble.

In some cases, such as rock climbing, this book will give you an introduction to some great places to go climbing, as well as some important information to know before you go. Rock climbing is a very specialized sport that requires commensurate gear and training. Take the time to check out some of the recommended resources this guidebook provides before engaging in such activities.

Err on the side of caution when pushing your limits, especially when in a wilderness situation. The elements don't care about your experience and fitness level. Listen to your gut about anything that doesn't feel right. Bring the essentials; let someone know where you're going and when you plan on being back. Obey regulations, pay the fees, abide kiosk signage, and don't make or leave a mess. We're living in a society. There are a lot of people moving to the Northwest. I was one of them eight years ago; you might be one too. Let's keep it nice for everyone who's here now and everyone who's coming. This place is far too special not to preserve it as is.

The Ten Essentials

It's important to have a very healthy respect for Mother Nature. Conditions in Oregon are notorious for changing rapidly and with little or no warning. The "expect the best but prepare for the worst" adage is a great thing to keep in mind when you're preparing to go into the wilderness, or even just hiking in Forest Park. Always let somebody know where you're going and when you plan on being back. Know your limitations, and, as already stated, err on the side of caution. If conditions of any sort are making you uncomfortable, that's a good sign to head back or take appropriate action.

Be prepared. Whether you are new to the outdoors or an Eagle Scout, the ten essentials are something that all hikers should have on hand. Here is a list of the updated essential "systems" for hikers, but cyclists and paddlers should consider these as well, particularly items 1, 2, 3, and 9.

1. **Navigation.** A map and a compass are mandatory. These can be augmented with things like altimeters and GPS units, but always have a map of the area and a compass.

2. **Sun protection.** Bring sunglasses, sunscreen, and proper clothing, including a hat.

3. **Insulation.** Will there be a blizzard on the Timberline Trail in July? Probably not. However, you should have whatever it takes to survive the worst conditions that can be reasonably expected. No matter the season, start your outfit with wicking gear: clothing that is not made of cotton and that can wick moisture away from the body. Dress in layers, especially in cooler weather. Pack extra socks. If things are going to be cold or wet, bring additional layers and rain gear. Whatever the conditions, avoid cotton.

SWEEPING VISTAS

Whatever your outdoor endeavor of choice may be, odds are you'd like the scenery to be attractive. If you're whitewater rafting, the fact that Portland is within driving distance of three designated Wild and Scenic Rivers has you covered with regards to pretty things to look at. If you're hiking, biking, or flatwater paddling, having a Cascade peak or four to gaze upon at some point in the outing can be a dangling carrot too good to pass up. Here are some of the area's best outdoor adventures with a view. Some of these are included in this book. Others I didn't have room for, but all are worth a mention up front simply for the outstanding views they offer.

Hiking McIntyre Ridge

Just an hour outside Portland, a trail ascends one of the westernmost ridges of the Cascades. The McIntyre Ridge offers grand vistas of everything from Portland to Mount Hood as it makes its way to the top of Wildcat Mountain. From early to midsummer, numerous wildflowers including lupine, Indian paintbrush, and rhododendron can be found along the trail of this 7-mile, 1,100-foot elevation gain hike. Bear grass and a stunning view of Mount Hood dominate the landscape as the ridge emerges from the forest.

From Portland, take US 26 East for 30 miles to Firwood Road. Turn right onto Firwood and continue a short distance until you reach a three-way stop. Turn right, continuing on Firwood through several turns until reaching

4. **Illumination.** Flashlights, headlamps, and LEDs all work. It's good to have a backup light source or spare batteries.

5. **First-aid supplies.** It's up to you whether to bring such things as allergy pills or latex gloves. At the very least you will need some gauze, bandages, tape, and pain meds. There are many prepackaged kits available that include everything from bare-bones basics to an outdoor aid station.

6. **Fire.** This includes waterproof matches, disposable lighters, and chemical heat tabs.

7. **Repair kit and tools.** A knife or multitool is fairly standard. Depending on what you're doing, duct tape and rope can be handy as well.

Wildflowers, dominated by bear grass, provide the foreground for a classic Mount Hood view.

Wildcat Mountain Road at a four-way stop. Turn left onto Wildcat Mountain Road (FR 36) for 8.9 miles until the road becomes FR 3626. Continue and at 9.4 miles you'll arrive at an unsigned fork, where the paved spur to the

8. **Nutrition.** Carry at least enough food for an extra day and night in the wilderness. Nutrition bars, jerky, nuts, and the like all work.

9. **Hydration.** Always bring at least a full water bottle or water bladder/reservoir system. You should also have some sort of water treatment or filtration on hand.

10. **Emergency shelter.** If you're backpacking, the tent you're carrying covers this one. If you're taking a day hike, consider a space blanket, rain gear, or even a trash bag.

Douglas Trail heads downhill and to the right. Turn right, and follow this paved spur, immediately going left at a second unmarked fork 100 yards from the first junction. The paved route climbs for a short distance before ending at the Douglas Trailhead.

Follow the McIntyre Ridge Trail for 2.2 miles to an open meadow complete with bench and views for a break. This is a good place to turn around if you're tired or have little hikers. To continue to Wildcat Mountain, head south for 0.5 mile to the junction with the Douglas Trail. Turn left and continue another 0.5 mile to a spur trail on the right. If you start heading downhill, you missed the turn. The 0.2-mile spur trail leads to the view from the top of Wildcat Mountain. Return the way you came.

Paddling Timothy Lake

A pristine lake in the middle of the forest with a Cascade peak in the background is a scene that's never going to disappoint. Sitting on the southwest side of Mount Hood, Timothy Lake, while man-made, is nonetheless a fantastic spot for taking in the mountain from the water. Mount Hood isn't visible

A kayaker enjoys the sun on Timothy Lake.

from every spot on the lake, but it's only 2 square miles of water, so paddle around to find the perfect view.

From Portland, take I-84 East to exit 16 and follow signs for US 26 East. Drive around Mount Hood and through Government Camp, making a right onto Oregon Skyline Road. Following signs for Timothy Lake, make a right on FR 57 and put in from either Oak Fork, Gone Creek, or Hood View Campground launch areas. For more information, check out adventure 33.

Hiking and Cycling Council Crest

Council Crest is the highest point in the city of Portland. Once home to an amusement park complete with roller coaster, the tiny, elevated parcel of land affords a sweeping view. The greater Portland area is laid out before you from this vantage, as well as Mounts Hood, Adams, and St. Helens and, just over her shoulder, Mount Rainier. Sure you can drive it, but how adventurous is that? Take a hike or a bike ride to the 1,071-foot crest. For directions, check out adventure 1 or 16.

Cycling Larch Mountain

One of the best views anywhere near Portland, Sherrard Point on Larch Mountain should be somewhere at the top of your hit list if that sort of thing matters to you in the slightest. The bike ride to the summit of the extinct volcano is an arduous one, no doubt about it. In terms of scenery, the ride is memorable in its own right. After arriving at the summit parking area, a quick walk up to the fenced Sherrard Point provides views of the Columbia River Gorge and every Cascade peak in the area, including Jefferson. For more information, check out adventure 5.

Hiking Silver Star Mountain

In no way, shape, or form easy to get to, the view from Silver Star Mountain—an exposed, twin-summited mountain in southwest Washington's Skamania County—is a stunner. It affords a 360-degree panorama that encompasses the Columbia River Gorge and the full complement of cascade volcanoes. It also boasts arguably the best wildflower show in the area, on display from mid-June through August.

The view from Ed's Trail on Silver Star Mountain

To get there from Battle Ground, head north on WA 503 for 5.5 miles; turn right onto SE Rock Creek Road. Drive 8.5 miles and turn right onto Sunset Falls Road. Continue another 7 miles to the Sunset Falls Campground. Make a right here and cross a bridge over the Lewis River. Just after the bridge, make a left onto FR 41 and travel 3.5 miles to a hard, downhill right onto FR 4109. Drive a rough 1.5 miles to another junction. Turn left here and drive the final 2.7 miles to the trailhead, at the end of the road.

A recommended route to the top is via Ed's Trail. Start hiking at the far (west) end of the parking area near the map kiosk. Follow the trail for 0.5 mile until it joins up with an old road and continues ascending. After 1 mile the road banks sharply up to the right. Just after this bank, turn left at the signed junction with Ed's Trail. The next 2 miles of hiking are epic. Walk through meadows, under a rock arch, and up a scrambly rock staircase. The trail eventually enters a forest before reaching a five-way junction. Turn left here onto a jeep road; make another left 200 yards later. Walk up this rocky road 0.25 mile to the twin summit. Trails lead up to each high point. Walk back down past the previous five-way junction. Stay on this old jeep road as it briefly ascends and then gently descends 2.7 miles back down to the trailhead parking area.

Hiking Saddle Mountain

Aptly named Saddle Mountain is the highest peak in northwest Oregon's Coast Range. The summit offers views that stretch from Astoria and the Pacific Ocean to the Cascade peaks of Mounts Rainier, Adams, St. Helens, and Hood. Someone also hauled everything they needed to assemble a picnic bench up there. The 6-mile, 1,700-foot elevation gain hike to the top is a favorite during the peak wildflower months of May and June.

Take US 26 West out of Portland for about 65 miles. Near milepost 10, make a hard right at the sign for Saddle Mountain State Park. Travel this narrow, winding road for 7 miles to the parking lot and trailhead at the end.

The hike starts uphill and after 0.2 mile comes to a side trail leading off to the right. Continue straight, climbing for 2 miles before arriving at open wildflower meadows. Shortly thereafter you get a view of the saddle and the final ascent to the summit. The last 0.5 mile is steep, but cables along the way offer some help and stability in the rougher parts. Head back the way you came.

The Saddle Mountain summit, with the Pacific Ocean in the distance

First Aid

I know you're tough, but get 10 miles into the woods and develop a blister and you'll wish you had carried that first-aid kit. Face it; it's just plain good sense. Many companies produce lightweight, compact first-aid kits. Just make sure yours contains at least the following:

- ❐ adhesive bandages
- ❐ moleskin or duct tape
- ❐ various sterile gauze and dressings
- ❐ white surgical tape
- ❐ an Ace bandage
- ❐ an antihistamine
- ❐ aspirin
- ❐ Betadine solution
- ❐ a first-aid book
- ❐ antacid tablets
- ❐ tweezers
- ❐ scissors
- ❐ antibacterial wipes
- ❐ triple-antibiotic ointment
- ❐ plastic gloves
- ❐ sterile cotton-tip applicators
- ❐ syrup of ipecac (to induce vomiting)
- ❐ thermometer
- ❐ wire splint

Here are a few tips for dealing with, and hopefully preventing, certain ailments.

Sunburn. Take along sunscreen or sunblock, protective clothing, and a wide-brimmed hat. If you do get a sunburn, treat the area with aloe vera gel and protect the area from further sun exposure. At higher elevations the sun's radiation can be particularly damaging to skin. Remember that your eyes are vulnerable to this radiation as well. Sunglasses can be a good way to prevent headaches and permanent eye damage from the sun, especially in places where light-colored rock or patches of snow reflect light up into your face.

Blisters. Be prepared to take care of these hike-spoilers by carrying moleskin (a lightly padded adhesive), gauze and tape, or adhesive bandages. An effective way to apply moleskin is to cut out a circle of moleskin and remove the center—like a doughnut—and place it over the blistered area. Cutting the center out will reduce the pressure applied to the sensitive skin. Other products can help you combat blisters. Some are applied to suspicious hot spots before a blister forms to help decrease friction to that area, while others are applied to the blister after it has popped to help prevent further irritation.

Insect bites and stings. You can treat most insect bites and stings by applying hydrocortisone 1 percent cream topically and taking a pain medication such as ibuprofen. If you forgot to pack these items, a cold compress or a paste of mud and ashes can sometimes assuage the itching and discomfort. Remove any stingers by using tweezers or scraping the area with your fingernail or a knife blade. Don't pinch the area; you'll only spread the venom.

Some people are highly sensitive to bites and stings and may have a serious allergic reaction that can be life threatening. Symptoms of a serious allergic reaction can include wheezing, an asthmatic attack, and shock. The treatment for this severe type of reaction is epinephrine. If you know that you are sensitive to bites and stings, carry a pre-packaged kit of epinephrine, which can be obtained only by prescription from your doctor.

Ticks. Ticks can carry diseases such as Rocky Mountain spotted fever and Lyme disease. The best defense is, of course, prevention. If you know you're going to be hiking through an area littered with ticks, wear long pants and a long-sleeved shirt. You can apply a permethrin-based repellent to your clothing and a DEET-based repellent to exposed skin. At the end of your hike, do a spot check for ticks. If you do find a tick, grab the head of the tick firmly—with a pair of tweezers if you have them—and gently pull it away from the skin with a twisting motion. Sometimes the mouth parts linger, embedded in your skin. If this happens, try to remove them with a disinfected needle. Clean the affected area with an antibacterial cleanser and then apply triple antibiotic ointment. Monitor the area for a few days. If irritation persists or a white spot or bull's-eye rash develops, see a doctor for possible infection.

Poison ivy, oak, and sumac. These skin irritants can be found most anywhere in North America and come in the form of a bush or a vine, having leaflets in groups of three, five, seven, or nine. Learn how to spot the plants. The oil they secrete can cause an allergic reaction in the form of blisters, usually about 12 hours after exposure. The itchy rash can last from ten days to several weeks.

The best defense against these irritants is to wear clothing that covers the arms, legs, and torso. For summer, zip-off cargo pants come in handy. There are also nonprescription lotions you can apply to exposed skin that guard against the effects of poison ivy/oak/sumac and can be washed off with soap and water. If you think you were in contact with the plants, after hiking (or even on the trail during longer hikes), wash with soap and water. Taking a hot shower with soap after you return home from your hike will also help remove any lingering oil from your skin. Should you contract a rash from any of these plants, use an antihistamine to reduce the itching. If the rash is localized, create a light bleach/water wash to dry up the area. If the rash has spread, either tough it out or see your doctor about getting a dose of cortisone (available both orally and by injection).

Snakebites. Snakebites are rare in North America. Unless startled or provoked, the majority of snakes will not bite. If you are wise to their habitats and keep a careful eye on the trail, you should be just fine. When stepping over logs, first step on the log, making sure you can see what's on the other side before stepping down. Though your chances of being struck are slim, it's wise to know what to do in the event you are.

If a nonvenomous snake bites you, allow the wound to bleed a small amount and then cleanse the wounded area with a Betadine solution (10 percent povidone-iodine). Rinse the wound with clean water (preferably) or fresh urine (it might sound ugly, but it's sterile). Once the area is clean, cover it with triple antibiotic ointment and a clean bandage. Remember, most residual damage from snakebites, venomous or otherwise, comes from infection rather than the bite itself. Keep the area as clean as possible and get medical attention immediately.

If somebody in your party is bitten by a venomous snake, follow these steps:

1. Calm the victim.
2. Remove jewelry, watches, and restrictive clothing, and immobilize the affected limb. Do not elevate the injury. Medical opinions vary on whether the area should be lower or level with the heart, but the consensus is that it should not be above it.
3. Make a note of the circumference of the limb at the bite site and at various points above the site as well. This will help you monitor swelling.
4. Evacuate the victim. Ideally he should be carried out to minimize movement. If the victim appears to be doing okay, he can walk. Stop and rest frequently.

If the swelling appears to be spreading or the victim's symptoms increase, change your plan and find a way to get the person transported.

5. If you are waiting for rescue, make sure to keep the victim comfortable and hydrated (unless he begins vomiting).

Snakebite treatment is rife with out-of-date and potentially dangerous remedies: You used to be told to cut the bite site and suck the venom out or use a suction-cup extractor for the same purpose; applying an electric shock to the area was even in vogue for a while. Do *not* do any of these things. Do not apply ice, do not give the victim painkillers, and do not apply a tourniquet. All you really want to do is keep the victim calm and get help. If you're alone and have to hike out, don't run—you'll only increase the flow of blood—and venom—throughout your system. Instead, walk calmly.

Dehydration. Have you ever hiked in hot weather and had a roaring headache and felt fatigued after only a few miles? More than likely you were dehydrated. Symptoms of dehydration include fatigue, headache, and decreased coordination and judgment. When you are hiking, your body's rate of fluid loss depends on a number of factors, including outside temperature, humidity, altitude, and your activity level. On average, a hiker walking in warm weather will lose 4 liters of fluid a day. That fluid loss is easily replaced by normal consumption of liquids and food. However, hikers walking briskly in hot, dry weather and hauling a heavy pack can lose 1 to 3 liters of water an hour. It's important to always carry plenty of water and to stop often and drink fluids regularly, even if you aren't thirsty.

Heat exhaustion is the result of a loss of large amounts of electrolytes and often occurs if a hiker is dehydrated and has been under heavy exertion. Common symptoms of heat exhaustion include cramping, exhaustion, fatigue, lightheadedness, and nausea. You can treat heat exhaustion by getting out of the sun and drinking an electrolyte solution made up of 1 teaspoon of salt and 1 tablespoon of sugar dissolved in 1 liter of water. Drink this solution slowly over a period of 1 hour. Drinking plenty of fluids (preferably an electrolyte solution/sports drink) can prevent heat exhaustion. Avoid hiking during the hottest parts of the day, and wear breathable clothing, a wide-brimmed hat, and sunglasses.

Hypothermia is one of the biggest dangers in the backcountry, especially for day hikers in the summertime. That may sound strange, but imagine starting out on a hike in midsummer when it's sunny and 80°F out. You're clad in nylon shorts and a cotton T-shirt. About halfway through your hike, the sky begins to cloud up; in the next hour a light drizzle begins to fall and the wind starts to pick up. Before you know it you are soaking wet and shivering—the perfect recipe for hypothermia. More-advanced symptoms include decreased coordination, slurred speech, and blurred vision. When a victim's temperature falls below 92°F, blood pressure and pulse plummet, possibly leading to coma and death.

To avoid hypothermia, always bring a windproof/rainproof shell, a fleece jacket, long underwear made of a breathable synthetic fiber, gloves, and a hat when you are hiking in the mountains. Learn to adjust your clothing layers based on the temperature. If you are climbing uphill at a moderate pace, you will stay warm; but when you stop for a break, you'll become cold quickly, unless you add more layers of clothing.

If a hiker is showing advanced signs of hypothermia, dress her in dry clothes and make sure she is wearing a hat and gloves. Place the person in a sleeping bag in a tent or shelter that will protect her from the wind and other elements. Give the person warm fluids to drink and keep her awake.

Frostbite. When the mercury dips below 32°F, your extremities begin to chill. If a persistent chill attacks a localized area, say, your hands or your toes, the circulatory system reacts by cutting off blood flow to the affected area—the idea being to protect and preserve the body's overall temperature. And so it's death by attrition for the affected area. Ice crystals start to form from the water in the cells of the neglected tissue. Deprived of heat, nourishment, and now water, the tissue literally starves. This is frostbite.

Prevention is your best defense against this situation. Most prone to frostbite are your face, hands, and feet, so protect these areas well. Wool is the traditional material of choice because it provides ample airspace for insulation and draws moisture away from the skin. Synthetic fabrics, however, have made great strides in the cold weather clothing market. Do your research. Wearing a pair of light silk liners under your regular gloves is a good trick for keeping warm. They afford some additional warmth, but more importantly they'll allow you to remove your gloves for dexterous work without exposing the skin.

If your feet or hands start to feel cold or numb due to the elements, warm them as quickly as possible. Place cold hands under your armpits or bury them in your crotch. If your feet are cold, change your socks. If there's plenty of room in your boots, add another pair of socks. Do remember, though, that constricting your feet in tight boots can restrict blood flow and actually make your feet colder more quickly. Your socks need to have breathing room if they're going to be effective. Dead air provides insulation. If your face is cold, place your warm hands over your face, or simply wear a head stocking.

Should your skin go numb and start to appear white and waxy, chances are you've got or are developing frostbite. Don't try to thaw the area unless you can maintain the warmth. In other words, don't stop to warm up your frostbitten feet only to head back on the trail. You'll do more damage than good. Tests have shown that hikers who walked on thawed feet did more harm, and endured more pain, than hikers who left the affected areas alone. Do your best to get out of the cold entirely and seek medical attention—which usually consists of performing a rapid rewarming in water for 20 to 30 minutes.

The overall objective in preventing both hypothermia and frostbite is to keep the body's core warm. Protect key areas where heat escapes, such as the top of the head, and maintain the proper nutrition level. Foods that are high in calories aid the body in producing heat. Never smoke or drink alcohol when you're in situations where the cold is threatening. By affecting blood flow, these activities ultimately cool the body's core temperature.

Altitude sickness (AMS). High lofty peaks, clear alpine lakes, and vast mountain views beckon hikers to the high country. But those who like to venture high may become victims of altitude sickness (also known as acute mountain sickness, or AMS). Altitude sickness is your body's reaction to insufficient oxygen in the blood due to decreased barometric pressure. While some hikers may feel lightheaded, nauseous, and experience shortness of breath at 7,000 feet, others may not experience these symptoms until they reach 10,000 feet or higher.

Slowing your ascent to high places and giving your body a chance to acclimatize to the higher elevations can prevent altitude sickness. For example, if you live at sea level and are planning a weeklong backpacking trip to elevations between 7,000 and 12,000 feet, start by staying below 7,000 feet for one night, then move to between 7,000 and 10,000 feet for another night or two. Avoid strenuous exertion and alcohol to give your body a chance to adjust to the new altitude. It's also important to eat light food and drink plenty of nonalcoholic fluids, preferably water. Loss of appetite at altitude is common, but you must eat!

Most hikers who experience mild to moderate AMS develop a headache and/or nausea, grow lethargic, and have problems sleeping. The treatment for AMS is simple: Stop heading uphill. Keep eating and drinking water, and take meds for the headache. You actually need to take more breaths at altitude than at sea level, so breathe a little faster without hyperventilating. If symptoms don't improve over 24 to 48 hours, descend. Once you descend about 2,000 to 3,000 feet, your symptoms will usually begin to diminish.

Severe AMS comes in two forms: high altitude pulmonary edema (HAPE) and high altitude cerebral edema (HACE). HAPE, an accumulation of fluid in the lungs, can occur above 8,000 feet. Symptoms include rapid heart rate, shortness of breath at rest, AMS symptoms, dry cough developing into a wet cough, gurgling sounds, flulike or bronchitis symptoms, and lack of muscle coordination. HAPE is life threatening, so descend immediately, at least 2,000 to 4,000 feet. HACE usually occurs above 12,000 feet but sometimes occurs above 10,000 feet. Symptoms are similar to HAPE but also include seizures, hallucinations, paralysis, and vision disturbances. Descend immediately—HACE is also life threatening.

Hantavirus pulmonary syndrome (HPS). Deer mice spread the virus that causes HPS, and humans contract it from breathing it in, usually when they've disturbed an area with dust and mice feces from nests or surfaces with mice droppings or urine. Exposure to large numbers of rodents and their feces or urine presents the greatest risk. As hikers, we sometimes enter old buildings, and often deer mice live in these places. We may not be around long enough to be exposed, but do be aware of this disease. About half the people who develop HPS die. Symptoms are flulike and appear about two to three weeks after exposure. After initial symptoms, a dry cough and shortness of breath follow. Breathing is difficult. If you even think you might have HPS, see a doctor immediately!

Trail Etiquette

Leave no trace. Always leave an area just as you found it—if not better than you found it. Avoid camping in fragile, alpine meadows and along the banks of streams and lakes. Use a camp stove versus building a wood fire. Pack out all your trash and extra food. Bury human waste at least 100 feet from water sources under 6 to 8 inches of topsoil. Don't bathe with soap in a lake or stream—use prepackaged moistened towelettes to wipe off sweat and dirt, or bathe in the water without soap.

Stay on the trail. It's true, a path anywhere leads nowhere new, but purists will just have to get over it. Paths serve an important purpose: They limit impact on natural areas. Straying from a designated trail may seem innocent, but it can cause damage to sensitive areas—damage that may take years to recover, if it can recover at all. Even simple shortcuts can be destructive. So, please, stay on the trail.

Leave no weeds. Noxious weeds tend to overtake other plants, which in turn affects animals and birds that depend on those plants for food. To minimize the spread of noxious weeds, hikers should regularly clean their boots, tents, packs, and hiking poles of mud and seeds. Also brush your dog to remove any weed seeds before heading off into a new area.

Keep your dog under control. You can buy a flexi-lead that allows your dog to go exploring along the trail, while allowing you the ability to reel him in should another hiker approach or should he decide to chase a rabbit. Always obey leash laws, and be sure to bury your dog's waste or pack it out in resealable plastic bags.

Respect other trail users. Often you're not the only one on the trail. With the rise in popularity of multiuse trails, you'll have to learn a new kind of respect, beyond the nod and "hello" approach you may be used to. First investigate whether you're on a multiuse trail, and assume the appropriate precautions. When you encounter motorized vehicles (ATVs, motorcycles, and 4WDs), be alert. Though they should always yield to the hiker, often they're going too fast or are too lost in the buzz of their engine to react to your presence. If you hear activity ahead, step off the trail just to be safe. Note that you're not likely to hear a mountain biker coming, so be prepared and know ahead of time whether you share the trail with them. Cyclists should always yield to hikers, but that's little comfort to the unwary hiker who gets run into. Be aware. When you approach horses or pack animals on the trail, always step quietly off the trail, preferably on the downhill side, and let them pass. If you're wearing a large backpack, it's often a good idea to sit down. To some animals, a hiker wearing a large backpack might appear threatening. Many national forests allow domesticated grazing, usually for sheep and cattle. Make sure your dog doesn't harass these animals, and respect ranchers' rights while you're enjoying yours.

Hiking with Children

Hiking with children isn't a matter of how many miles you can cover or how much elevation gain you make in a day; it's about seeing and experiencing nature through their eyes.

Kids like to explore and have fun. They like to stop and point out bugs and plants, look under rocks, jump in puddles, and throw sticks. If you're taking a toddler or young child on a hike, start with a trail you're familiar with. Trails that have interesting things for kids, like piles of leaves to play in or a small stream to wade through during the summer, will make the hike much more enjoyable for them and will keep them from getting bored.

You can keep your child's attention if you have a strategy before starting on the trail. Using games is not only an effective way to keep a child's attention but also a great way to teach him or her about nature. Quiz children on the names of plants and animals. Pick up a family-friendly outdoor hobby like geocaching (geocaching.com) or letterboxing (atlasquest.com), both of which combine the outdoors, clue solving, and treasure hunting. If your children are old enough, let them carry their own daypack filled with snacks and water. So that you are sure to go at their pace and not yours, let them lead the way. Playing follow the leader works particularly well when you have a group of children. Have each child take a turn at being the leader.

With children, bringing a lot of clothing is key. The only thing predictable about weather is that it will change. Especially in mountainous areas, weather can change dramatically in a very short time. Always bring extra clothing for children, regardless of the season. In winter have your children wear wool socks and warm layers, such as long underwear, a fleece jacket and hat, wool mittens, and good rain gear. It's not a bad idea to have these along in late fall and early spring as well. Good footwear is also important. A sturdy pair of high-top tennis shoes or lightweight hiking boots is the best bet for little ones. If you're hiking in summer near a lake or stream, bring along a pair of old sneakers that your child can put on when he wants to go exploring in the water. Remember when you're near any type of water, always watch your child at all times. Also, keep a close eye on teething toddlers, who may decide a rock or leaf of poison oak is an interesting item to put in their mouth.

From spring through fall, you'll want your kids to wear a wide-brimmed hat to keep their face, head, and ears protected from the hot sun. Also, make sure your children wear sunscreen at all times. Choose a brand without PABA—children have sensitive skin and may have an allergic reaction to sunscreen that contains PABA. If you are hiking with a child younger than 6 months, don't use sunscreen or insect repellent. Instead, be sure the child's head, face, neck, and ears are protected from the sun with a wide-brimmed hat, and that all other skin exposed to the sun is protected with the appropriate clothing.

Remember that food is fun. Kids like snacks, so it's important to bring a lot of munchies for the trail. Stopping often for snack breaks is a fun way to keep the trail interesting. Raisins, apples, granola bars, crackers and cheese, cereal, and trail mix all make great snacks. Also, a few of their favorite candy treats can go a long way toward heading off a fit of fussing. If your child is old enough to carry her own backpack, let her fill it with some lightweight "comfort" items, such as a doll, a small stuffed animal, or a little toy (you'll have to draw the line at bringing the 10-pound Tonka truck). If your kids don't like drinking water, you can bring some powdered drink mix or a juice box.

Avoid poorly designed child-carrying packs—you don't want to break your back carrying your child. Most child-carrying backpacks designed to hold a 40-pound child will contain a large carrying pocket to hold diapers and other items. Some have an optional rain/sun hood.

Hiking with Your Dog

Bringing your furry friend with you is always more fun than leaving him behind. Our canine pals make great trail buddies because they never complain and always make good company. Hiking with your dog can be a rewarding experience, especially if you plan ahead.

Getting your dog in shape. Before you plan outdoor adventures with your dog, make sure he's in shape for the trail. Getting your dog into shape takes the same discipline as getting yourself into shape; luckily, your dog can get in shape with you. Take your dog with you on your daily runs or walks. If there is a park near your house, hit a tennis ball or play Frisbee with your dog.

Swimming is also an excellent way to get your dog into shape. If there is a lake or river near where you live and your dog likes the water, have him retrieve a tennis ball or stick. Gradually build your dog's stamina up over a two- to three-month period. A good rule of thumb is to assume that your dog will travel twice as far as you will on the trail. If you plan on doing a 5-mile hike, be sure your dog is in shape for a 10-mile hike.

Training your dog for the trail. Before you go on your first hiking adventure with your dog, be sure he has a firm grasp on the basics of canine etiquette and behavior. Make sure he can sit, lie down, stay, and come. One of the most important commands you can teach your canine pal is to "come" under any situation. It's easy for your friend's nose to lead him astray or possibly get him lost. Another helpful command is the "get behind" command. When you're on a narrow hiking trail, you can have your dog follow behind you when other trail users approach. Nothing is more bothersome than an enthusiastic dog that runs back and forth on the trail and disrupts the peace of the trail for others—or, worse, jumps up on other hikers and gets them muddy. When you see other trail users approaching you on the trail, give them the right of way by quietly stepping off the trail and making your dog lie down and stay until they pass.

Equipment. The most critical pieces of equipment you can invest in for your dog are proper identification and a sturdy leash. Flexi-leads work well for hiking because they give your dog more freedom to explore but still leave you in control. Make sure your dog has identification that includes your name and address and a number for your veterinarian. Other forms of identification for your dog include a tattoo or a microchip. You should consult your veterinarian for more information on these last two options.

The next piece of equipment you'll want to consider is a pack for your dog. By no means should you hold all of your dog's essentials in your pack—let him carry his own gear! Dogs that are in good shape can carry 30 to 40 percent of their own weight.

Most packs are fitted by a dog's weight and girth measurement. Companies that make dog packs generally include guidelines to help you pick out the size that's right for your dog. Some characteristics to look for when purchasing a pack for your dog include a harness that contains two padded girth straps, a padded chest strap, leash attachments, removable saddle bags, internal water bladders, and external gear cords.

You can introduce your dog to the pack by first placing the empty pack on his back and letting him wear it around the yard. Keep an eye on him during this first introduction. He may decide to chew through the straps if you aren't watching him closely. Once he learns to treat the pack as an object of fun and not a foreign enemy, fill the pack evenly on both sides with a few ounces of dog food in resealable plastic bags. Have your dog wear his pack on your daily walks for a period of two to three weeks. Each week add a little more weight to the pack until your dog will accept carrying the maximum amount of weight he can carry.

You can also purchase collapsible water and dog food bowls for your dog. These bowls are lightweight and can easily be stashed into your pack or your dog's. If you are hiking on rocky terrain or in the snow, you can purchase footwear for your dog that will protect his feet from cuts and bruises.

Always carry plastic bags to remove feces from the trail. It is a courtesy to other trail users and helps protect local wildlife.

The following is a list of items to bring when you take your dog hiking: collapsible water bowls, a comb, a collar and a leash, dog food, plastic bags for feces, a dog pack, flea/tick powder, paw protection, water, and a first-aid kit that contains eye ointment, tweezers, scissors, stretchy foot wrap, gauze, antibacterial wash, sterile cotton-tip applicators, antibiotic ointment, and cotton wrap.

First aid for your dog. Your dog is just as prone—if not more prone—to getting in trouble on the trail as you are, so be prepared. Here's a rundown of the more likely misfortunes that might befall your little friend.

Bees and wasps. If a bee or wasp stings your dog, remove the stinger with a pair of tweezers and place a mudpack or a cloth dipped in cold water over the affected area.

Porcupines. One good reason to keep your dog on a leash is to prevent him from getting a nose full of porcupine quills. You may be able to remove the quills with pliers, but a veterinarian is the best person to do this nasty job because most dogs need to be sedated.

Heat stroke. Avoid hiking with your dog in really hot weather. Dogs with heat stroke will pant excessively, lie down and refuse to get up, and become lethargic and disoriented. If your dog shows any of these signs on the trail, have him lie down in the shade. If you are near a stream, pour cool water over your dog's entire body to help bring his body temperature back to normal.

Heartworm. Dogs get heartworms from mosquitoes, which carry the disease in the prime mosquito months of July and August. Giving your dog a monthly pill prescribed by your veterinarian easily prevents this condition.

Plant pitfalls. One of the biggest plant hazards for dogs on the trail are foxtails. Foxtails are pointed grass seed heads that bury themselves in your friend's fur, between his toes, and even get in his ear canal. If left unattended, these nasty seeds can work their way under the skin and cause abscesses and other problems. If you have a long-haired dog, consider trimming the hair between his toes and giving him a summer haircut to help prevent foxtails from attaching to his fur. After every hike, always look over your dog for these seeds—especially between his toes and his ears.

Other plant hazards include burrs, thorns, thistles, and poison oak. If you find any burrs or thistles on your dog, remove them as soon as possible, before they become an unmanageable mat. Thorns can pierce a dog's foot and cause a great deal of pain. If you see that your dog is lame, stop and check his paws for thorns. Dogs are immune to poison oak, but they can pick up the sticky, oily substance from the plant and transfer it to you.

Protect those paws. Be sure to keep your dog's nails trimmed so he avoids getting soft tissue or joint injuries. If your dog slows and refuses to go on, check to see that his paws aren't torn or worn. You can protect your dog's paws from trail hazards such as sharp gravel, foxtails, lava scree, and thorns by purchasing dog boots.

Sunburn. If your dog has light skin, he is an easy target for sunburn on his nose and other exposed skin areas. You can apply a nontoxic sunscreen to exposed skin areas that will help protect him from overexposure to the sun.

Ticks and fleas. Ticks can easily give your dog Lyme disease, as well as other diseases. Before you hit the trail, treat your dog with a flea-and-tick spray or powder. You can also ask your veterinarian about a once-a-month pour-on treatment that repels fleas and ticks.

Mosquitoes and deerflies. These little flying machines can do a job on your dog's snout and ears. Spraying your dog with fly repellent for horses will discourage both pests.

Giardia. Dogs can get giardia, which results in diarrhea. It is usually not debilitating, but it's definitely messy. A vaccine against giardia is available.

Mushrooms. Make sure your dog doesn't sample mushrooms along the trail. They could be poisonous to him, but he doesn't know that.

When you are finally ready to hit the trail with your dog, keep in mind that national parks and many wilderness areas do not allow dogs on trails. Your best bet is to hike in national forests, Bureau of Land Management (BLM) lands, and state parks. Always call ahead to see what the restrictions are.

Map Legend

Municipal

≡⟨84⟩≡	Interstate Highway
≡⟨30⟩≡	Featured US Highway
≡⟨30⟩≡	US Highway
≡⟨120⟩≡	Featured State Road
≡⟨120⟩≡	State Road
≡⟨83⟩≡	Featured Local/Forest Road
≡⟨83⟩≡	Local/Forest Road
====	Gravel Road
====	Unpaved Road
⊢—+—⊣	Railroad
-----	State Boundary
•—•—•—•	Power Line

Trails

▬▬▬	Featured Paved Trail
———	Paved Trail
▬ ▬ ▬	Featured Trail
- - - -	Trail

Symbols

⊃⊂	Bridge
⬐	Boat Launch
▪	Building/Point of Interest
▲	Campground
∧	Cave
⏚⏚⏚	Cliff
—	Dam
⌖	Gate
▲	Mountain Peak
🅿	Parking
⤓	Put-in/Takeout
🛉🛉	Restrooms
⬤	Rock Formation
⬕	Scenic View
○	Town
①	Trailhead
❓	Visitor/Information Center

Water Features

	Body of Water
	Marsh
	River/Creek
	Intermittent Stream
≋	Waterfall

Land Management

▣	National Park/Forest
▣	National Wilderness/Recreation Area
▣	State Park/Forest, County/City Park
⬚	National Scenic Area

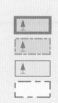

CYCLING

Portland is a bike town. There are more bicycle commuters per capita here than any other US city. There are bike lanes, bike boxes (at an intersection a section of a traffic lane designated as a visible and safe area where bicyclists can wait out a red light), and designated bike routes. We are home to the nation's largest naked bike ride and, coming in summer 2016, a bike share program. Beyond the city's commuter-based attributes, the area's nature and accompanying scenery all but beg to be taken in at a pace slower than that afforded by an automobile. Whether you're looking for thrilling in-city rides, thigh-burning climbs, flat pedals, rolling hills, technical singletrack, or all of the above, it's here.

An optional stop on the Forest Park Loop, the St. Johns Bridge affords great views of a number of Cascade peaks on a clear day.

Recommended Outfitters and Guide Services

Cycle Portland Bike Tours. Offering gear rentals and tours, Cycle Portland Bike Tours is a great single-stop option (portlandbicycletours.com).

LifeCycle Adventures. Providing custom bike tours all over the state, LifeCycle Adventures covers everything from gear and logistical support to lodging and food. Whether you want to go around Mount Hood or through the Columbia River Gorge, explore wine country, or anything else, they provide the best experience possible (lifecycleadventures.com).

Pedal Bike Tours. If you want to see Portland via bicycle, these folks are tops. They offer a number of tours including city, brewery, and food cart tours. And all the gear you need is provided (pedalbiketours.com).

Adventure 1: Council Crest–Washington Park Loop

The Council Crest–Washington Park Loop combines the thrill of riding through the streets of "Bike Town USA" with the exercise and exhilaration of a thigh-burning climb to the highest point in Portland. Along the way you'll take in arguably the best view in the city and ride through iconic Washington Park. If you had one bike ride to check out Portland proper, this should be it.

Start: Broadway, Pioneer Courthouse Square (PCS)

Distance: 15.7-mile loop

Riding time: 1.5 to 2 hours

Best bike: Road bike

Terrain and trail surface: Paved

Traffic and hazards: Significant traffic downtown; less traffic around Council Crest, but blind turns and narrower roads

Fees and permits: None

Restrooms: At visitor center inside PCS

Maps: *Oregon Road & Recreation Atlas:* Page 106 D4

Getting there: However you get downtown to Pioneer Courthouse Square. GPS: N45° 31.144' / W122° 40.785'

The Ride

Starting in Pioneer Courthouse Square (PCS) in downtown Portland, you'll essentially be checking out the best of Portland by bicycle. As the ride begins, you'll have the opportunity to pedal your way through a downtown area that caters to bicyclists. With clearly marked bike routes, wide bike lanes, and bike boxes, it's a joy to explore a city laid out for folks on two wheels.

Once you hit Terwilliger Boulevard, the traffic lightens and the natural beauty becomes more pronounced. A steady but scenic climb eventually delivers you to the highest point in the city. On a clear day you can check out no fewer than four Cascade peaks and a sweeping view of the Rose City.

From Council Crest enjoy a well-earned mini-descent before leveling out and riding along very pleasant, tree-lined Hewett Boulevard.

A cyclist takes a breather at Council Crest, with Mount Hood in the background.

Take one more big breath and take on a mild ascent up Skyline before hitting Fairview and enjoying the downhill fruits of your labor. You'll now be descending through Washington Park, and if you're so inclined, there's an awful lot to see and do here: the zoo, Children's Museum, World Forestry Center, Japanese Garden, International Rose Test Garden. You get the idea. Once through the park the downhill segment continues through one of the stateliest neighborhoods in the city before arriving back downtown and concluding the loop.

Miles and Directions

0.0   Start at PCS and head south (uphill) on Broadway.

0.8   Keep left to stay on Broadway.

0.9   Slight right onto SW 6th Avenue.

1.0   Continue onto SW Terwilliger Boulevard.

1.3   Turn left to stay on Terwilliger.

3.4   Turn right onto SW Westwood Drive.

4.0   Turn right to stay on SW Westwood Drive.

Council Crest–Washington Park Loop

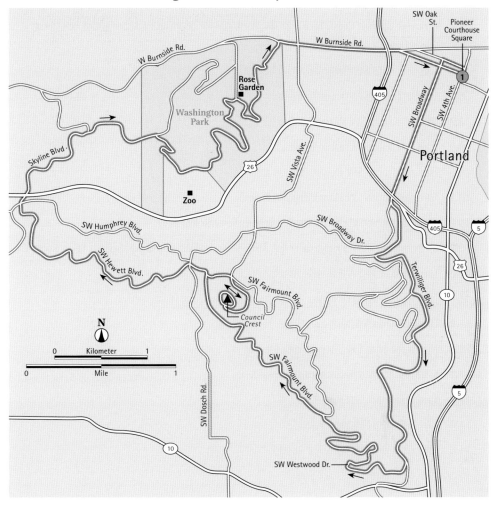

4.8   Turn left onto SW Westwood View.

4.9   SW Westwood View heads left and becomes Mitchell Street.

5.2   Turn left on SW Fairmount Boulevard.

5.7   Stay left on Fairmount.

6.2   Turn left to stay on Fairmount.

6.7   Turn right onto SW Talbot Terrace.

6.9   Turn right onto SW Greenway Avenue.

7.1	Turn right onto SW Council Crest Drive.
7.3	Turn right again on SW Council Crest Drive.
7.4	Arrive at Council Crest. Take a break; continue around and back down Council Crest Drive.
7.8	Turn left onto SW Greenway Avenue.
8.0	Turn left onto SW Talbot Terrace.
8.2	Continue onto SW Talbot Road.
8.3	Turn left onto SW Patton Road.
8.5	Turn right onto SW Hewett Boulevard.
10.1	Turn right onto SW Humphrey Boulevard.
10.2	Make an immediate left onto SW Scholls Ferry Road.
10.2	Make an immediate right, veer left, then stay straight, to stay on Scholls Ferry Road.
11.0	Turn right onto SW Fairview Boulevard.
11.6	Turn right onto SW Knights Boulevard.
11.8	Turn left onto SW Kingston Drive.
13.4	Turn right onto SW Sherwood Boulevard.
14.1	Slight right onto Sacajawea Boulevard.
14.3	Turn right onto SW Park Place.
14.4	Turn left onto SW Vista Avenue.
14.5	Turn right onto W Burnside Road.
15.2	Turn right onto SW Stark Street.
15.5	Turn right onto SW Broadway.
15.7	Arrive back at PCS.

Local Information

Things to see: Pioneer Courthouse Square, downtown Portland, Council Crest, sweeping views of Cascade peaks, zoo, Children's Museum, World Forestry Center, Japanese Garden, International Rose Test Garden

Restaurants along the ride: Food carts at SW 9th and Alder; the Imperial, 410 SW Broadway; beers at Bailey's Taproom, 213 SW Broadway, all in Portland

Adventure 2: Willamette River Loop

The Willamette River Loop is a mostly flat ride that offers a chance to check out the city's south side. You'll get some excellent views along segments of river bike paths and cruise by the towns of Milwaukie, Oregon City, and Lake Oswego. You'll climb past Tryon Creek State Park and descend down a winding, beautiful, and vista-laden Terwilliger Blvd before finishing in Portland's waterfront.

Start: Governor Tom McCall Waterfront Park

Distance: 29.7-mile loop

Riding time: 1.5 to 3 hours

Best bike: Road bike

Terrain and trail surface: Paved road, bike path

Traffic and hazards: High pedestrian traffic along the waterfront bike path areas; lots of cars on OR 43

Fees and permits: None

Restrooms: None at trailhead; plenty along the route

Maps: *Oregon Road & Recreation Atlas:* Page 106 D4

Getting there: From downtown Portland, head east to the waterfront. Make a right on 1st Avenue. If you're driving, park somewhere near 1st Avenue and Main Street and head 1 block east to the Tom McCall Waterfront Park. GPS: N45° 31.113' / W122° 40.766'

The Ride

From Tom McCall Waterfront Park, head south on the Waterfront Park path. You'll cross under the Hawthorne Bridge and then pedal across it as you make your way over the Willamette and onto Portland's east side. In short order you'll make your way past the Oregon Museum of Science & Industry and underneath the spanking-new Tilikum Crossing Bridge.

Don't let the immediate views on the Springwater Corridor dampen your spirit. Once you pass under the Ross Island bridge, the city is behind you and the views of the Willamette really open up. The riding is easy here as you ride past the Oaks Bottom Wildlife Refuge, Oaks Amusement Park, and Sellwood Riverfront Park.

You'll rejoin the world of automotive traffic as you enter Milwaukie. If you have the time and inclination, visit the downtown area across 99E from

Downtown Portland as seen from the east side of the Willamette River

Milwaukie Waterfront Park. It's quite charming. After skirting Milwaukie the ride pulls away from the Willamette River and heads toward the Clackamas River. After crossing it you'll be treated to some nice views of the Clackamas before passing under I-205 and heading down Main Street in Oregon City. This is another great place to explore if you have the time. The end of the Oregon Trail, charming Oregon City has a lot to offer culturally.

Crossing the Willamette one more time, the ride now starts back toward Portland along OR 43. Perhaps the least-inspiring portion of the loop, OR 43 offers little in the way of views and can be heavy on the traffic. All that changes, however, once you reach Old River Drive, where views and peace are restored.

After crossing Oswego Creek you'll be back on OR 43 briefly, but here's another chance to visit one of the area's explorable hamlets. Lake Oswego can easily and pleasantly eat up an afternoon if you let it, so be forewarned.

After another brief dalliance with OR 43, the ride becomes more scenic and peaceful as the only real ascent of the loop begins up Terwilliger Boulevard. There are no river views to be had here, but you'll be right alongside Tryon Creek State Park, so you'll have plenty of trees to look at. After the long climb, the descent

The loop takes you along the Willamette River.

back into downtown is beautiful, albeit seemingly brief. Now back where you started, the loop is officially over. But Veritable Quandary is right around the corner—and 30 miles earns you food and drink in my book.

Miles and Directions

0.0 Start at Tom McCall Waterfront Park near SW Main Street and Naito Parkway; head south along the bike path and under the Hawthorne Bridge.

0.2 Make a right onto the path leading up onto the Hawthorne Bridge.

0.5 After crossing the bridge, make a right onto the bike ramp leading down to the East Bank Esplanade.

0.6 Make a left at the bottom of the ramp.

1.0 Make a left where the path ends and follow the bike lane on SE Caruthers Street.

1.1 Make a right onto SE 4th Avenue.

1.2 Continue onto the Springwater Corridor.

4.4 Turn left onto SE Umatilla Street.

Willamette River Loop

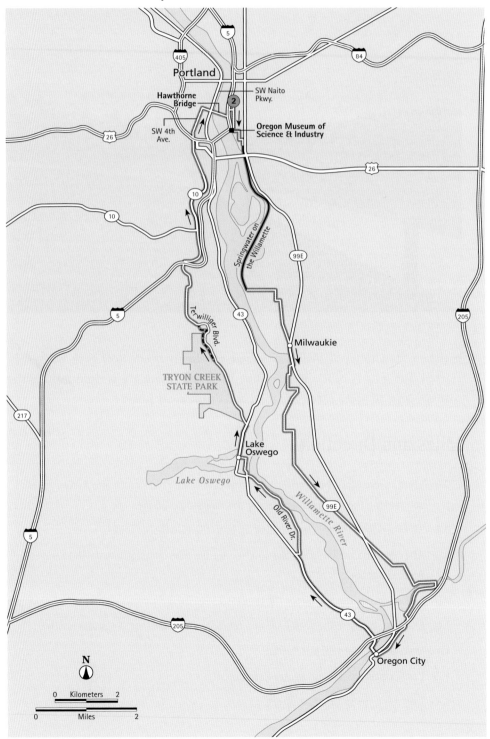

4.9 Turn right onto SE 16th Avenue.

5.2 Turn left onto Linn Avenue.

5.3 Turn right onto 17th Avenue.

6.3 Make a right onto the sidewalk at SE McLoughlin Boulevard and follow the bike path into the waterfront park.

6.8 Bike path ends, continue straight onto SE 19th Avenue.

7.1 Turn left onto SE Sparrow Street.

7.3 Stay right at the stop sign.

7.4 Turn left onto SE 23rd Avenue.

7.6 Make a left onto Park Avenue.

7.8 Turn right onto the Trolley Trail bike path.

8.4 Continue onto SE Arista Drive.

9.0 Continue onto the bike path that begins again on the left.

11.2 The bike path ends. Continue onto SE Abernethy Lane.

12.1 Make a right onto Portland Avenue.

12.5 Turn left onto Clackamas Boulevard.

13.0 At 82nd Avenue make a right onto the pedestrian bridge over the river.

13.2 Make a right and pick up the bike path.

14.1 Turn left onto Main Street.

15.1 Turn right onto 7th Avenue.

15.5 Pass under I-205; continue onto OR 43.

17.7 About 100 yards beyond Mapleton Drive, look for an easy-to-miss gap in the railing on the right. Pass through this and continue onto Old River Drive.

19.6 Take the access path on the right.

19.9 Cross a pedestrian bridge.

20.0 Turn right onto Furnace Street.

20.3 Turn left onto Leonard Street.

20.4 Turn right onto OR 43.

21.1 Turn left onto Terwilliger Boulevard.

29.3 Turn right onto SW Salmon Street.

29.7 Arrive back at Tom McCall Waterfront Park.

Local Information

Things to see: River views of the Willamette, Oregon Museum of Science & Industry (OMSI), Tryon Creek State Park, Portland waterfront

Restaurants along the ride: Rice Thai Cookery, 10614 SE Main St., Milwaukie; Ranee's on Main, 1003 Main St., Oregon City; Veritable Quandary, 1220 SW 1st Ave., Portland waterfront

Adventure 3: Forest Park Loop

The quadrant labeled Northwest Portland is known primarily for high-end shopping, with the dining options to match. It's also tucked right up against the base of the Tualatin Mountains. Mountains come in many shapes and sizes, however. And the Tualatins struggle to reach more than 1,000 feet. So keep that number in mind when you think, I'm ascending into a mountain range!? In addition to Washington Park and Council Crest, the Tualatins are where Forest Park stretches out, providing the natural backdrop Portland is known for. The Forest Park Loop will give you a taste of Portland's Northwest neighborhood and an ample sampling of the city's iconic park.

Start: Terminus of NW Thurman Street

Distance: 23.6-mile loop

Riding time: 1.5 to 3 hours

Best bike: Road bike

Terrain and trail surface: Paved road

Traffic and hazards: Swift-moving traffic on US 30; winding road with blind turns on Skyline Boulevard

Fees and permits: None

Restrooms: None at the trailhead

Maps: *Oregon Road & Recreation Atlas:* Page 106 D4

Getting there: From northwest Portland, take NW Thurman Street to its terminus at the trailhead. GPS: N45° 32.349' / W122° 46.521'

The Ride

The ride starts through a remarkably pleasant tree-lined neighborhood with little to no elevation gain over the first 2 miles. Once you begin the steady climb up NW Cornell Road, the elevation increases at a rate that keeps up with the escalating property values. As you continue the climb, the scenery transitions from the stately manors of the west hills to the natural beauty of bigleaf maple, Douglas fir, and western red cedar.

At about the 3-mile mark, the ride levels out briefly at the Audubon Society of Portland. If time is not an issue, this is a very worthwhile stop. The property is home to a 150-acre nature sanctuary, wildlife care center, and nature store, where you can pick up a copy of *Hiking Waterfalls in Oregon* if you're interested.

Heading down Germantown Road in Forest Park

Back on the road, the climbing continues on NW Skyline Boulevard before finally leveling out for good around the 7-mile mark. Enjoy the well-earned breather and the scenery as you skirt along the borders of the park. If you feel like pulling the chute early, you can knock off 7 miles of the ride by hanging a right onto NW Germantown Road. The winding, scenic descent is a thriller that ends with sweeping views of the St. Johns Bridge and Mount Hood, weather permitting. If you're in for the whole ride, continue to NW Newberry Road, where you'll make a right and begin your descent.

Once again at the base of the Tualatin Mountains, begin the flat, 7-mile time trial through the Northwest industrial area and back to the trailhead. Admittedly, the scenery along US 30 isn't as good as what you just left behind, but the flat ride back in makes for a nice cooldown.

Miles and Directions

0.0   Start at the trailhead and ride back along NW Thurman Street.

Forest Park Loop

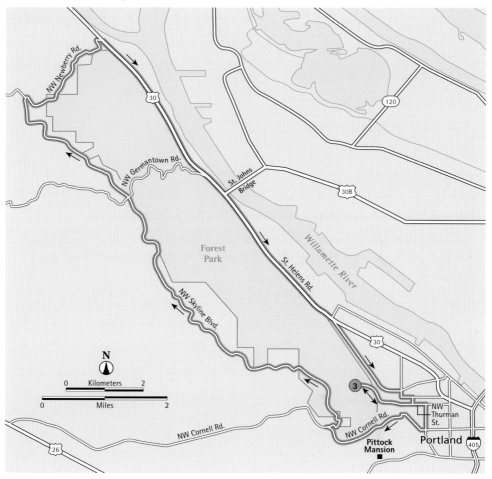

1.3   Turn right onto NW 25th Avenue.

1.7   Turn right onto NW Lovejoy Street.

1.8   Turn right onto NW Cornell Road.

3.6   Turn right onto NW 53rd Drive.

5.5   Turn right onto NW Thompson Road.

6.1   Turn right onto NW Skyline Boulevard.

12.4 Turn right onto NW Newberry Road.

14.5 Turn right onto US 30/St. Helens Road.

20.5	Turn right to stay on St. Helens Road.
22.0	Continue onto NW Nicolai Street.
22.2	Turn right onto NW Warday.
22.3	Continue onto NW Vaughn Street.
22.4	Turn right onto NW 27th Avenue.
22.5	Turn right onto NW Thurman Street.
23.6	Arrive back at the trailhead.

Local Information

Things to see: Forest Park, Audubon Society, St. Johns Bridge, Willamette River

Pre- and post-ride restaurants: Pre-ride coffee and breakfast at St. Honore Bakery, 2335 NW Thurman St.; post-ride beers and food at Lucky Lab, 1945 NW Quimby St., both in Portland

Adventure 4: North Portland Loop

The Portland peninsula bills itself as the "Gateway to nature." What many Portlanders consider to be one of the farthest, tumbleweed-laden, lawless outposts of the Rose City is in reality a fine place to get a little fresh air via bicycle. From the bluffs of Willamette Boulevard to the serene Smith and Bybee Lakes, there's a lot to appreciate on this 18.4-mile bike ride around North Portland.

Start: Kenton Park on N Brandon Avenue

Distance: 18.4-mile loop

Riding time: 1 to 3 hours

Best bike: Road bike

Terrain and trail surface: Paved road and bike path

Traffic and hazards: High traffic on Lombard Street

Fees and permits: None

Restrooms: Kelley Point Park, Smith and Bybee Wetlands Natural Area

Maps: *Oregon Road & Recreation Atlas:* Page 106 C4

Getting there: From downtown Portland, take I-5 North to exit 302C and merge onto North Greeley Avenue. Turn right onto Lombard Street and left onto North Brandon Street. Kenton Park will be on the left. If you're taking the MAX from downtown, hop on the yellow line heading toward the Expo Center; get off at the Kenton/Denver Avenue stop. The loop begins right there on Denver Avenue. GPS: N45° 35.010' / W122° 41.347'

The Ride

Due to the nature of a loop ride, you can start at a myriad of spots. But if you're traveling to North Portland, a great way to begin is by taking the MAX to the Kenton Station and beginning your journey there. From the charming downtown area of Kenton, head north on Denver Avenue for a quick 0.5 mile to the Columbia Slough Trail. Heading west, the paved path leads away from traffic along the tree-lined slough. You'll pass the Heron Lakes Golf Club and head north on the paved path paralleling North Portland Road. The Smith and Bybee Lakes are off to your left here, shielded from view by trees.

At the 3-mile mark you'll turn left onto a bike path that gets you even closer to the lakes, delivering you to the official Smith and Bybee Wetlands Natural

The view of downtown Portland from Willamette Boulevard

Area. If you feel like taking a leg stretch, there are restrooms here, as well as a few pedestrian-only paths with interpretive signs that lead through the wetlands.

Continuing on the paved path, now paralleling North Marine Drive, you spit back out onto the road around the 6.5-mile mark and almost immediately arrive at the entrance to Kelley Point Park. Unless you're crunched for time, take a ride along the paved path that loops through the park. This is where the Willamette and Columbia Rivers join forces, and it's another nice spot to stretch your legs or visit the restroom.

Once outside of the park, the main road becomes North Lombard Street. Shortly after it changes to North Columbia Boulevard, look for a paved bike path on the right leading into Chimney Park. Take this path through the park and over a pedestrian bridge into Pier Park. Continue through Pier Park and back out onto Lombard. Next up is the St. Johns neighborhood. Once its own town before Portland swallowed it up, St. Johns is heavy on charm, and the little main street is worth checking out. In addition, Portland's best bridge is here. Look right on North Philadelphia Avenue as you pedal through town to catch a glimpse.

After St. Johns the loop makes its way onto Willamette Boulevard, where you'll be treated to views of Forest Park, the Willamette River, the University of Portland, and, if conditions are right, sweeping views of downtown and Mount

Hood. Willamette banks a hard left and becomes Rosa Parks Way. A left onto Denver Avenue brings you back into Kenton and completes the loop.

Miles and Directions

0.0 Start from Kenton Park and head east on North McClellan Street.

0.1 Left onto North Denver Avenue.

0.1 Bear left at the Paul Bunyan statue to stay on Denver.

0.5 Take a path to the right that circles under the MAX bridge and head east on North Schmeer Road. Be mindful of oncoming traffic.

0.7 Take the paved path on the left onto the Columbia Slough Trail.

2.4 Follow the path as it turns to the right and parallels North Portland Road.

3.1 Use the crosswalk to cross North Portland Road and pick up the bike path on the other side of barricade.

4.1 The bike path exits the Smith and Bybee Wetlands. Stay on the paved path.

6.5 The path ends at North Marine Drive. Carefully cross the road and make a left.

6.5 Make a right onto North Kelley Point Park Road. Make loop around Kelley Point Park.

8.6 Make a right onto North Lombard Street.

8.9 Cross Lombard onto the paved sidewalk/bike path.

10.4 Cross Lombard and bike over the bridge in the bike lane.

10.9 Continue onto North Columbia Boulevard.

11.3 Take the paved bike path into Chimney Park.

11.6 Take the pedestrian overpass bridge. Stay on path through Pier Park and around the baseball field.

11.5 Turn left onto North James Street.

12.2 Turn right onto North St. Johns Avenue.

12.5 Turn left onto North Lombard Street.

13.4 Turn right onto North Richmond Avenue.

13.6 Turn left onto North Willamette Boulevard.

16.7 Make a hard left onto North Rosa Parks Way.

North Portland Loop

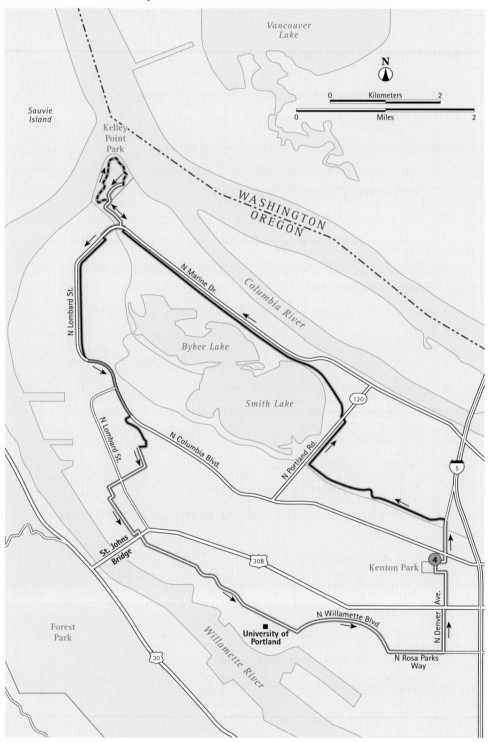

17.3   Turn left onto North Denver Avenue.

18.3   Turn left onto North McClellan Street.

18.4   Arrive back at Kenton Park.

Local Information

....

Things to see: Willamette River, University of Portland, Kelley Point Park, Smith and Bybee Lakes

Restaurants along the ride: PoShines, 8139 N Denver Blvd., Kenton; Signal Station Pizza, 8302 N Lombard St., St Johns

Adventure 5: Larch Mountain

The classic 45.4-mile round-trip ride from the Lewis and Clark State Recreation Site in Troutdale to the summit of the Larch Mountain Crater is not a casual Sunday leg stretch. A mettle-testing, 3,800-foot climb through exemplary Northwest forest is the primary reason for the ride. That being said, there are a handful of postcard-worthy views along the way, capped by a 360-degree, jaw-dropping panorama at Sherrard Point, the summit of the Larch Mountain Crater. On a clear day victorious riders can claim views of Mounts Rainier, St. Helens, Adams, and Hood among the visual rewards for their efforts.

Start: Lewis and Clark State Recreation Site in Troutdale

Distance: 45.4 miles out and back or 22.7-mile shuttle

Riding time: 3 to 5 hours

Best bike: Road bike

Terrain and trail surface: Paved road

Traffic and hazards: Somewhat busy in summer; some blind turns on the ascent

Fees and permits: None

Restrooms: At the trailhead, Vista House, and Sherrard Point

Maps: *Oregon Road & Recreation Atlas:* Page 107 D9

Getting there: From Portland, take I-84 East to exit 18. Take a left onto the Crown Point Highway. After 0.2 mile, turn into the Lewis and Clark State Recreation Site, on the left. GPS: N45° 32.453' / W122° 22.758'

The Ride

From Troutdale the ride begins innocently enough with an easy pedal along the Sandy River. The next 9 miles ascends along a low-traffic segment of the Historic Columbia River Highway at a relatively pleasant grade, passing scenic farmland and through the small town of Corbett before arriving at a must-see viewpoint at the Portland Women's Forum at the 8-mile mark. Looking east into the heart of the Columbia River Gorge, a number of Northwest landmarks make an appearance from this vantage, including Beacon Rock, the Vista House, Hamilton Mountain, and the highpoint of your ride, Larch Mountain.

At 8.5 miles you could stay left for a quick 0.5-mile side trip to the Vista House for a restroom break and a water refill if needed. Continuing the journey,

Ascending through the Larch Mountain Corridor

the big elevation gain now begins as you veer off onto Larch Mountain Road. Over the next 14 miles, you'll earn your supper. The climb steepens and never relents. But the beauty of the Larch Mountain Corridor will take your mind off your burning lungs and leg muscles . . . to some degree at least. The road ends at the Larch Mountain Crater parking area. But the climbing isn't done. Stash your bike and climb a long set of stairs to Sherrard Point. If you don't make this extra trip, you'll be kicking yourself the next day—the view is perhaps the best in the entire Columbia River Gorge National Scenic Area. Eat lunch, rehydrate, and head back the way you came.

Miles and Directions

0.0   Start from the recreation site parking area and turn left onto the Crown Point Highway.

4.3   Turn left onto East Bell Road.

5.5   Continue onto East Historic Columbia River Highway.

Larch Mountain

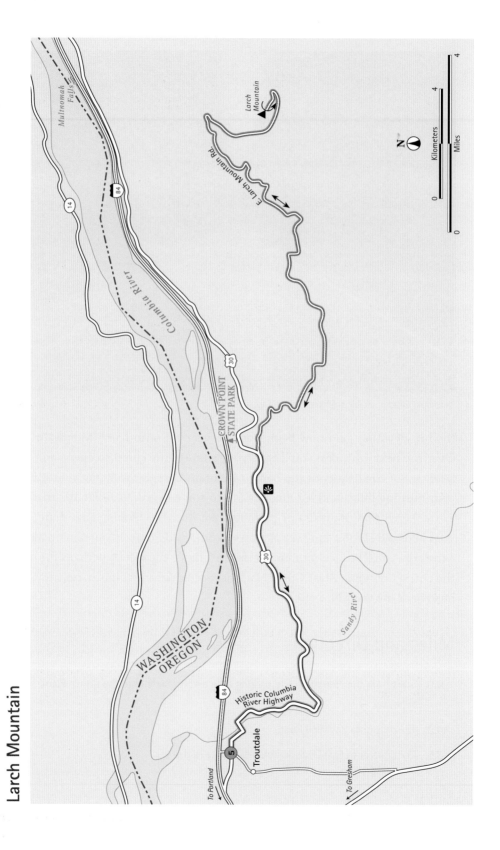

THE INTERTWINE

The Intertwine Alliance is a coalition of 140-plus public, private, and nonprofit organizations working to integrate nature more deeply into the Portland–Vancouver metropolitan region.

According to their website, the Intertwine:

- Drives the region's economy and tourist trade
- Preserves significant natural areas for wildlife habitat and public use
- Enhances the region's air and water quality
- Promotes citizens' health, fitness, and personal well-being
- Connects the region's communities with trails and greenways
- Provides sense of place and community
- Achieves equity, including racial equity
- Supports an ecologically sustainable metropolitan area
- Supports residents in lifelong learning about and stewardship of nature
- Reduces, mitigates, and helps us adapt to climate change

For more information, including a wonderful interactive map, visit theintertwine.org.

8.5 Bear right onto East Larch Mountain Road.

22.7 Arrive at the Larch Mountain Parking area. Take a quick hike up to Sherrard Point. If you haven't arranged for a shuttle, return the way you came.

45.4 Arrive back at the Lewis and Clark State Recreation Site.

Local Information

Things to see: The Columbia River Gorge and a handful of Cascade peaks from one of the best viewpoints in the area

Restaurants along the ride: Tad's Chicken 'n Dumplings, 1325 E Historic Columbia River Hwy., Troutdale

Adventure 6: Leif Erikson Drive

When it was constructed, Leif Erikson Drive was supposed to be the main artery that would connect Northwest Portland to a yet-to-be-constructed development of stately homes along the Tualatin Mountains. The combination of a massive landslide and a slumping economy prevented any further development. Investors defaulted, and the land fell back into the city's lap. That entire stretch of land is now Forest Park. And the road that was supposed to lead to high-end real estate now carves an easy path that winds its way from Northwest Portland to Germantown Road in the heart of the park.

Start: Leif Erikson Trailhead at the end of NW Thurman Street

Distance: 21.4 miles out and back (10.7-mile shuttle)

Riding time: 1 to 3 hours

Best bike: Mountain bike

Terrain and trail surface: Wide gravel road

Traffic and hazards: Pedestrians, hikers, runners, dogs

Fees and permits: None

Restrooms: None

Maps: *Oregon Road & Recreation Atlas:* Page 106 D4

Getting there: From downtown Portland, take I-405 North and take exit 3 onto US 30 West. Merge onto NW Vaughn Street. Turn left onto NW 26th Avenue. Make a right onto NW Thurman Street and follow it for 1.2 miles to the end of the road and the gated trailhead. GPS: N45° 32.346' / W122° 43.519'

The Ride

From the trailhead make your way past the gate and onto the gravel road. From there follow your nose. There is a little elevation gain to start with, but for the most part the entire ride is level and winding, with occasional rolling elevation gains and losses.

The path ducks in and out of canyons through a typical forest of Douglas fir, western red cedar, hemlock, bigleaf maple, and vine maple. Trails and fire lanes occasionally intersect Leif Erikson, so pay special attention and be on the lookout for hikers and runners at these junctions. Also be forewarned that this can be a muddy track, prone to puddles and standing water after any precipitation at all.

A cyclist enjoys Leif Erickson Drive.

Turn around where Leif Erikson ends at NW Germantown Road, or continue as far as you like. If you'd rather not come back the way you came and don't mind a little road riding, you have some options. At 6 miles a gravel road on your right, NW Saltzman Road, eventually becomes a paved NW Saltzman Road that intersects US 30. Hang a right there and make another right onto NW St. Helens Road; you'll be back in Northwest in no time. You can also do the same thing at Germantown Road by heading downhill to US 30.

Miles and Directions

0.0   Start at the trailhead and begin riding along gravel Leif Erikson Drive.

6.0   Pass NW Saltzman Road.

10.7   Arrive at NW Germantown Road. Head back the way you came.

21.4   Arrive back at the trailhead.

Leif Erikson Drive

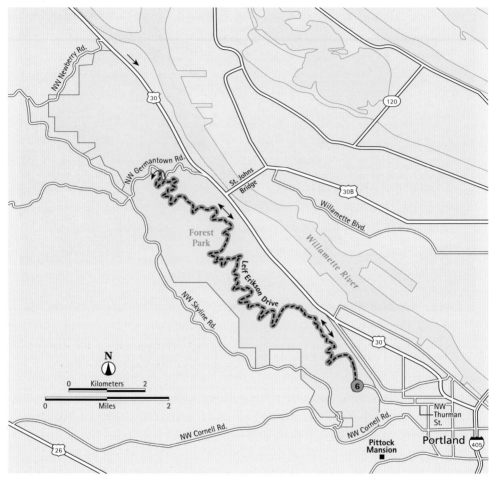

Local Information:

Things to see: Forest Park

Post-pedal food and drink: Rae's Lakeview Lounge, 1900 NW 27th Ave., Portland

Adventure 7: Springwater Corridor

One of the city's true gems, the Springwater Corridor travels roughly 22 miles from Portland to the hamlet of Boring along what used to be a rail line. With just a few exceptions, the well-graded ride is away from street traffic and is quite scenic and relatively peaceful. The path visits numerous parks along the route, making it a great option for visiting Portland's green spaces. A good part of the ride parallels Johnson Creek, crisscrossing it several times over bridges.

> Start: Oregon Museum of Science & Industry (OMSI)
>
> Distance: 43 miles out and back (21.5-mile shuttle)
>
> Riding time: 2 to 5 hours
>
> Best bike: Road bike
>
> Terrain and trail surface: Paved bike path
>
> Traffic and hazards: Pedestrians, potential for horses, occasional road crossings
>
> Fees and permits: None
>
> Restrooms: None at either trailhead
>
> Maps: *Oregon Road & Recreation Atlas:* Page 106 D5
>
> Getting there: Drive across the Hawthorne Bridge and make a right onto SE Water Avenue. Park in the OMSI parking lot, on the right. A paved path in the southwest corner of the parking lot leads to the East Bank Esplanade. GPS: N45° 30.470' / W122° 39.855'

The Ride

The ride down the Springwater Corridor goes from industrial to scenic in a hurry. In less than a mile, you'll leave behind the box buildings of 4th Avenue and pedal peacefully along the Willamette. Momentarily pulling away from the water view, the path bisects the Oaks Bottom Wildlife Refuge before passing the Oaks Amusement Park.

After 3.5 miles the trail pulls away from the Willamette for good and cuts through the neighborhood of Sellwood. And there's nothing wrong with that. After traversing the tree-lined streets of Sellwood, the paved path picks up again and crosses over busy McLoughlin Boulevard before almost vanishing into a lush valley that delivers you to and crosses over Johnson Creek for the first time. The path dances with Johnson Creek briefly and then comes back into contact with

The Springwater Corridor bends its way through the town of Milwaukie.

Springwater Corridor

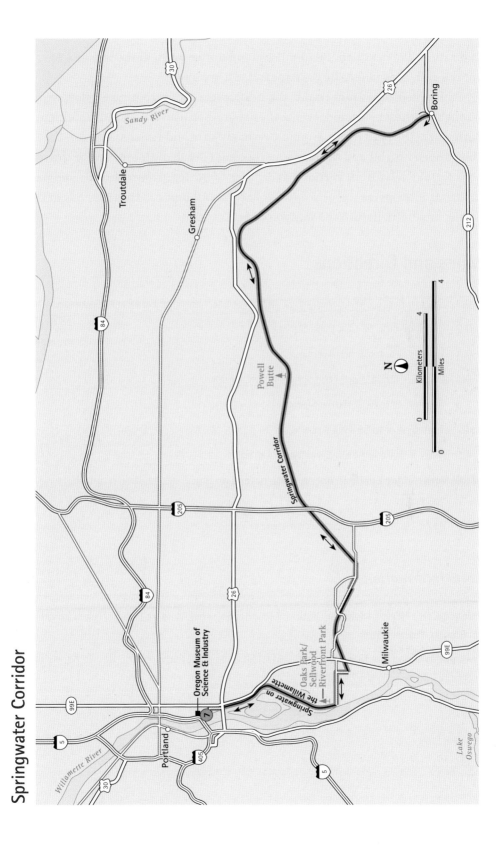

civilization. The next handful of miles doesn't offer much in the way of scenery, but the path does ramble by Cartlandia if you're hungry.

Still tucked away from traffic, the next several miles continue a slow weave through southeast Portland, eventually passing between Powell Butte and Jenne Butte Park. The path bends around Gresham Butte and revisits Johnson Creek. Things open up a bit and the landscape becomes decidedly more rural as the ride pulls farther away from Portland and closer to Boring. Views of fields and pasturelands intersperse the occasional collection of homes as the ride ends at the Boring Trailhead. Return the way you came.

Miles and Directions

0.0   Start from the OMSI parking area and make a left onto the East Bank Esplanade.

0.2   Continue onto SE Caruthers Street.

0.3   Turn right onto SE 4th Avenue.

0.5   Continue straight onto the Springwater Corridor.

3.5   Turn left onto SE Umatilla Street.

4.2   Turn right onto SE 19th Avenue.

4.5   Make a sharp left onto Springwater Corridor.

21.5   Arrive at the Boring Trailhead. If you haven't arranged for a shuttle, return the way you came.

43.0   Arrive back at the OMSI parking area.

Local Information

Things to see: Tideman Johnson Natural Area, Beggars-Tick Wildlife Refuge, Leach Botanical Garden, Powell Butte

Restaurants along the ride: Cartlandia, 8145 SE 82nd Ave., Portland; The Not So Boring Bar and Grill, 28014 SE Wally Rd., Boring

Adventure 8: Banks–Vernonia Trail

The nonprofit Rails-to-Trails Conservancy has the enviable task of converting former rail lines into trails. The first conservancy project in Oregon, the 8-foot-wide, 21-mile Banks–Vernonia Trail extends from the town of Banks, in Washington County, to the town of Vernonia in the Coast Range. The multiuse trail is open to bicyclists, walkers, and runners and is paralleled by a 4-foot-wide horse path. The ride cuts through canopied second-growth forest and open meadows and visits a pair of 80-foot-high railroad trestles. There are six separate trailheads spread out along the length of the trail. All the trailheads can be reached by car, and most provide restrooms, picnic tables, and Americans with Disabilities Act (ADA) access.

Start: Banks Trailhead

Distance: 42 miles out and back (21-mile shuttle). Multiple trailheads along the route make it extremely customizable.

Riding time: 2 to 5 hours

Best bike: Road bike

Terrain and trail surface: Paved bike path

Traffic and hazards: Occasional road crossings, pedestrians, potential for horses

Fees and permits: None

Restrooms: At the trailheads

Maps: *Oregon Road & Recreation Atlas:* Page 35 E8

Getting there: From Portland, take US 26 West to NW Banks Road. Make a right and then a quick left onto NW Banks and a right onto NW Sellers Road into the trailhead parking area. GPS: N45° 37.343' / W123° 6.859'

The Ride

From the Banks Trailhead, the first 5 miles of the trail are flat, with much of the ride paralleling US 26, which admittedly isn't much fun for anybody. After that the trail pulls away into the woods and begins a steady but manageable climb just before the Buxton Trestle at the 6.5-mile mark. The restored 80-foot-high, 700-foot-long railroad trestle now serves as one of the highlights of the ride. It's certainly worth pulling over for a couple of photos here.

Continuing past another trailhead, the path reenters the forest and stays that way as the ascent continues. The scenery continues unblemished until just before the 10-mile mark. Things open up at another trailhead at Stub Stewart

The restored 700-foot-long Buxton Trestle is one of the highlights of the ride.

State Park. Just after you cross NW Nowakowski Road, the climbing ends after 11 total miles of riding.

Enjoy a gentle descent to the next trailhead at OR 47. The mellow loss of elevation continues as things stay primarily forested before spitting you out at a meadow at 13.5 miles. The path levels off and visits a series of clustered woods followed by open meadows. The trail eventually meets back up with OR 47 and parallels it for the rest of the journey, finally arriving at the Vernonia Trailhead. Return the way you came.

Miles and Directions

0.0   Start at the Banks Trailhead.

21.0   Arrive at the Vernonia Trailhead. Connect with your shuttle, or return the way you came.

42.0   Arrive back at the Banks Trailhead.

Banks–Vernonia Trail

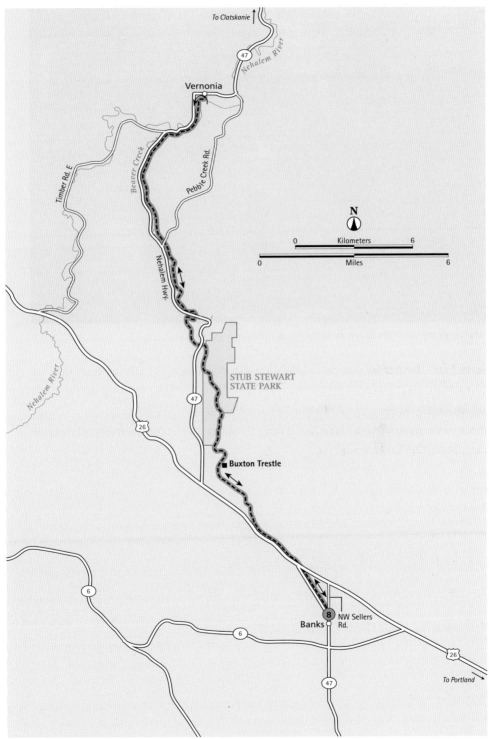

A canopied segment of the Banks–Vernonia Trail

Local Information

Things to see: Buxton and Horseshoe Trestles, Stub Stewart State Park

Restaurants along the ride: Main Street Pizza Company, 680 S Main St., Banks; Blue House Cafe, 919 Bridge St., Vernonia

Adventure 9: Hood River to Mosier Trail

This 9-mile, out-and-back ride along a restored section of the Historic Columbia River Highway in Hood River makes for a great weekend leg stretch for yourself or an outing with the family. The wide, paved path offers views of the Columbia River Gorge that are almost constant and always breathtaking.

Start: Mark O. Hatfield Trailhead in Hood River

Distance: 9.0 miles out and back

Riding time: 1 to 2 hours

Best bike: Road bike or mountain bike

Terrain and trail surface: Wide paved trail

Traffic and hazards: Somewhat heavy pedestrian use, particularly on weekends

Fees and permits: Northwest Forest Pass or day-use fee

Restrooms: At the trailhead

Maps: *Oregon Road & Recreation Atlas*: Page 37 12D

Getting there: From Hood River, drive east on State Street, crossing the Hood River and arriving at a four-way stop. Continue straight onto Old US 30. The road begins a steep, winding ascent, becoming Old Columbia River Drive and arriving a short time later at the trailhead. GPS: N45° 42.222' / W121° 29.225'

The Ride

From the Mark O. Hatfield Trailhead in Hood River, this paved restored segment of the Historic Columbia River Highway parallels the river for 4.5 miles to the east trailhead. The path winds gently along basalt cliffs and beneath forest canopies. Along the route there are viewpoint pullouts and remnants of the Old Historic Highway, perfect spots for a water or snack break. There are a couple of minor, rolling ascents and descents that will provide some exercise, but nothing too strenuous.

After about 4 miles of pedaling, the trail enters the Mosier Twin Tunnels. The restored tunnels were part of the original construction of the "King of Roads" back in 1919, and they make a great carrot to dangle in front of kids who are not in the mood to get on a bike. Windows within the tunnels, carved out of the basalt, look down to the river below.

A mix of beauty, history, and relative ease make this outing exemplary for families or new riders working on conditioning. In addition, there is the added

Riding through the Mosier Twin Tunnels

bonus of biking in a transition zone. Because the path is located where the river eases through the Cascade Range, it showcases flora from both the lush western side as well as the more arid eastern side. The mix is beautiful. Bear in mind that the Gorge is notorious for wind and weather conditions that change rapidly. Check conditions before you go, but be prepared for hot in summer and rainy in winter. There's a good chance there will be wind whenever you go.

The trail is popular among bicyclists as well as walkers, hikers, and joggers, many of whom have dogs along for the journey, so watch your speed, particularly through the tunnels. The trail ends at the east trailhead shortly after the tunnels, the turnaround point for this outing.

Miles and Directions

0.0 Start at the Mark O. Hatfield Trailhead.

4.5 Arrive at the east trailhead. Head back the way you came.

9.0 Arrive back at the trailhead.

Hood River to Mosier Trail

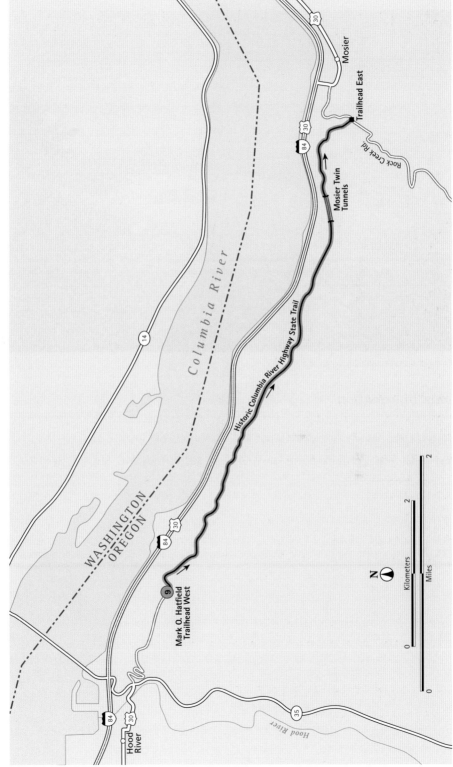

The view of the Columbia River from the trail

Local Information

....

Things to see: The Columbia River Gorge and the Mosier Twin Tunnels

Post-pedal food and drink: Priem Family Brewers, 797 Portway Ave., Ste. 101, Hood River

Adventure 10: Powell Butte

Singletrack options can be a bit scarce within Portland's city limits. One beaming exception is Powell Butte. It might not provide the miles of singletrack offered over at Sandy Ridge, but there's enough variety and sharp descents to hold your attention. Trails transition quickly from open meadows into tight, western red cedar–lined singletrack. Unlike some other city parks, most of the trails at Powell Butte are bike friendly.

Start: SE Ellis Street and 145th Avenue

Distance: 4.4-mile loop

Riding time: 0.5 to 2 hours

Difficulty rating: Easy to intermediate

Trail surface: Singletrack, dirt roads, asphalt, gravel

Elevation gain: Maximum single gain of 350 feet

Land status: City park

Hours: 5 a.m. to 10 p.m.

Seasons: Best July through Oct; trails closed in muddy conditions

Nearest town: Portland

Other trail users: Hikers, equestrians

Canine compatibility: Leashed dogs permitted

Wheels: Suspension recommended

Fees and permits: None

Restrooms: At visitor center

Maps: *Oregon Road & Recreation Atlas:* Page 107 E7

Special considerations: Please be respectful and adhere to bike restrictions on the Dogwood-Holgate, Dogwood, Fernwood, and Hawthorn Trails, as well as Reservoir Lane. Everything else is open season. Also bear in mind that many trails on Powell Butte have recently been renamed, so make sure you acquire an up-do-date map online or stop by the visitor center to familiarize yourself with the layout. There's also an updated map placard at the trailhead.

Getting there: Take SE Holgate Boulevard east to SE 136th Avenue. Turn right onto SE 136th Avenue and then left onto SE Ellis Street. Ellis Street turns to the right and becomes SE 145th Avenue; park here. The paved entry to the park on the Cedar Grove Trail is on the east side of the street. GPS: N45° 28.932' / W122° 30.876'

The Ride

From the Cedar Grove Trailhead, ride a quick 0.1 mile to where the trail forks. From this point Powell Butte becomes a choose-your-own adventure. For the described route, turn left at the fork and begin a slow, steady ascent up the Cedar Grove Trail. After 0.5 mile of total riding, you'll reach a junction with the Elderberry Trail. A hard left onto the Elderberry Trail is a completely viable option, but for now continue straight as the Cedar Grove Trail joins the Elderberry Trail. Shortly thereafter you'll reach a T junction at Meadowland Lane. Turn right here and enjoy the now-level trail and views of Mount Hood and Mount St. Helens.

After a little over 1 mile of total riding, you'll have another decision to make. At a four-way junction you can either go left or straight to ride Summit Lane or turn right onto the Douglas Fir Trail. Save the trip down Douglas Fir for later, and this time continue straight onto Summit Lane. Pass a junction with the Hawthorn Trail, not open to bikes, and make a right at the next junction with the South Trail. The descent begins mildly at first but picks up steam after a large hairpin turn.

A biker makes his way down the Douglas Fir Trail.

Descending through the trees

Powell Butte

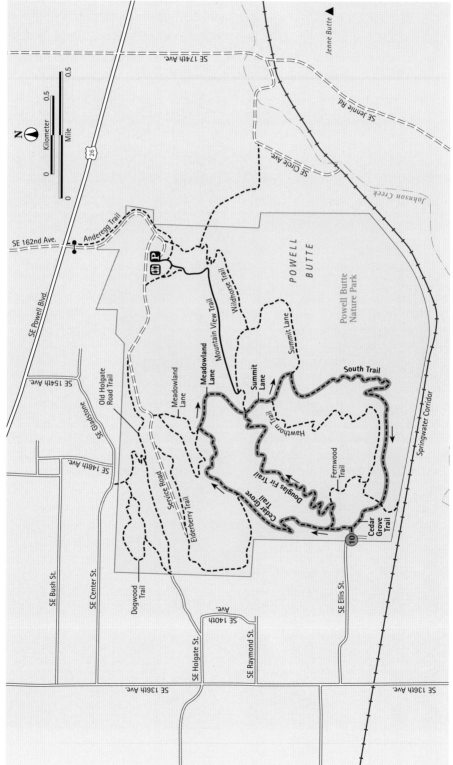

The path continues downward as it straightens out. Make a right onto the Cedar Grove Trail and then another right onto the Douglas Fir Trail and begin the curved, forested ascent of the butte. At the top you'll encounter a familiar junction. Turn right onto Summit Lane, and then right again to head down the South Trail a second time. This go-round you'll stay straight at the junction with the Hawthorn Trail, continuing onto the Cedar Grove Trail. When the Cedar Grove Trail splits, turn left and arrive back at the trailhead. If you prefer straighter ascents and winding descents, you can run the course in reverse, going up the South Trail and down the Douglas Fir Trail.

Miles and Directions

0.0   Start on the paved path onto the Cedar Grove Trail.

0.1   Make a left, staying on the Cedar Grove Trail.

0.5   Stay straight onto the Elderberry Trail.

0.85 Make a right onto Meadowland Lane.

1.1   Stay straight onto Summit Lane.

1.3   Turn right onto the South Trail.

2.2   Make a right onto the Cedar Grove Trail and stay straight for 0.2 mile, passing a junction leading back to the trailhead and arriving at a junction with the Douglas Fir Trail.

2.4   Make a right onto the Douglas Fir Trail.

3.1   Turn right onto Summit Lane.

3.3   Turn right onto the South Trail.

4.2   Make a right onto the Cedar Grove Trail.

4.3   Turn left to stay on the Cedar Grove Trail.

4.4   Arrive back at the trailhead.

Local Information

Post-pedal food and drink: La Costita, 17102 SE Powell Blvd., Portland

Adventure 11: Lumberyard Indoor Bike Park

The Lumberyard is the Northwest's premier indoor bike park. And while you might not be able to enjoy the outdoor aspects of biking in an indoor park, sometimes warm and dry trumps wet and freezing. The Lumberyard caters to all skill levels, including those whose wheels have never touched a trail. The environment is friendly and inclusive and has just about everything you could ever want to improve your skills: jump lines, pump tracks, skill sections, and areas for technical riding.

Start: 2700 NE 82nd Ave.

Distance: Self-dependent

Riding time: Self-dependent

Difficulty rating: Easy to difficult

Trail surface: Mostly wood, ramps; some technical spots

Elevation gain: NA

Land status: Private business

Seasons: All

Nearest town: In Portland

Other trail users: NA

Canine compatibility: Dogs not permitted

Wheels: Any

Fees and permits: Admission fee

Maps: *Oregon Road & Recreation Atlas:* Page 106 C6

Getting there: From downtown Portland, take I-84 East to exit 5. Make two rights to get on 82nd Avenue northbound. Drive 0.8 mile to the Lumberyard Indoor Bike Park at 2700 NE 82nd Ave. GPS: N 45° 32.482' / W 122° 34.668'

The Ride

The Lumberyard is a great place. You're just as likely to see a 7-year-old coasting by casually as you are a 20-something daredevil with 4 percent body fat pulling a backflip off a ramp—and literally everything in between. They are open year-round but are a magnificent option when it gets ugly outside. Even the hard-core crowd can have a difficult time getting up for a ride in harsh weather. If you want to keep your skills polished, get some exercise, or even improve your chops, this is the place to do it.

Kids making good use of the Lumberyard

The Lumberyard offers programs, skill-building clinics, equipment rentals, bike storage, summer camps, after-school programs . . . even beer and food! There's a basement street course and ramps outside. The staff is always helpful and more than willing to give you a rundown on anything and everything in the place. The initial draw to a place like the Lumberyard might be to hide from the weather, but after a visit or two, you might decide to incorporate it into all seasons.

Adventure 12: Sandy Ridge

Sandy Ridge is located west of Mount Hood in a forest populated by Douglas fir, western hemlock, and western red cedar. Specifically designed for mountain bikers, the recently expanded Sandy Ridge Trail System offers over 15 miles of bike paths. Sandy Ridge has something for every skill level, from easy-flow runs to extremely difficult technical trails with exposure. The trails dip and weave through a classic Northwest forest, but they are anything but typical. Built with assistance from the International Mountain Biking Association, the layout and maintenance of the trails is top-notch. Highlights include Flow Motion, an intermediate flow trail with no fewer than fifteen berms, and Follow the Leader, a double black diamond segment with exposure and big grade reversals.

Start: Sandy Ridge Trailhead

Distance: 12.6-mile loop

Riding time: 1 to 3 hours

Difficulty rating: Easy to extremely difficult

Trail surface: Singletrack, dirt roads

Elevation gain: 1,900 feet

Land status: BLM land

Seasons: All

Nearest town: Sandy

Other trail users: Hikers

Canine compatibility: Leashed dogs permitted but not recommended

Wheels: Suspension recommended

Fees and permits: None; donations appreciated

Maps: *Oregon Road & Recreation Atlas*: Page 36 H6

Special considerations: Stay on the trails. This trail system is located on the southern boundary of the Bull Run Watershed. Entering the watershed is punishable under federal law. The BLM has installed a donation tube at the Sandy Ridge Trailhead, with every dollar going to trail maintenance. It's a great trail system. Please consider making a donation if you use it.

Getting there: From Portland, take US 26 East. Make a left onto East Sleepy Hollow Drive in Sandy. Take the next right onto East Barlow Trail Road and follow it across the Sandy River; keep right at the immediate intersection. Continue past the first parking area and restroom. The trailhead is signed about 0.25 mile ahead, on the left. Unpaved parking is available near the yellow gate at Homestead Road. GPS: N45° 22.836' / W122° 1.825'

The Ride

From the trailhead begin up Homestead Road, passing the easy Homestead Loop. Pass a junction with the Hide and Seek Trail and continue the steady ascent up Homestead Road. Continue past the Hide and Seek Cutoff and the outlet for Flow Motion, eventually arriving at the information board at the top of the ridge. From here it's all downhill, and you've got options.

The big fun, and also the most challenging run, is down the double black diamond Follow the Leader. It starts out innocently enough, descending gently through scree fields. After crossing a creek things get real in a hurry as the bottom drops out from beneath you. Turns get tight here. The path seems intent on getting you down to the bottom, and throws in some eye-widening exposure, rock overhangs, and grade reversals for fun.

The warmup trail from the parking area at Sandy Ridge.

But for this ride, head down the Rock Drop, a black diamond trail with, you guessed it, a series of rock drops and rollers. Exit the Rock Drop onto Communication Breakdown. The intermediate trail meanders a bit before visiting a pair of epic viewpoints and settling into nonstop berms before spitting you out onto Quid Pro Flow. Rollable and leapable, the black diamond trail is prime for jumps. After getting your fill of air, the trail levels out and comes to a junction with Three Thirty Eight.

Things stay pretty level through this section of the Three Thirty Eight loop as you make your way to a junction with Two Turntables and a Microwave. Yet another black diamond trail, Two Turntables welcomes you with a rock drop and a handful of quick berms. The descent steepens and the path gets a little drifty before it connects with Hide and Seek. Hide and Seek begins its life at the top of the ridge as a tight, quick-moving black diamond that mellows out after the intersection with Two Turntables. What is left of Hide and Seek by the time you enter here is an easy, forested downhill to the trailhead. But that comes later.

For now, you're only taking Hide and Seek to get back to Homestead Road and then Flow Motion. As fun as they come, the intermediate trail is a seemingly endless flow. Berms and rollers, followed by rollers and berms, get you back down to Homestead Road and the cutoff over to the bottom portion of Hide and Seek.

Miles and Directions

0.0 Start at the trailhead and head up Homestead Road.

4.0 Arrive at a ridge summit. Head down Rock Drop.

4.5 Continue onto Communication Breakdown.

6.0 Turn right onto Quid Pro Flow.

7.2 Turn right onto Three Thirty Eight.

7.7 Turn right onto Two Turntables and a Microwave.

8.9 Turn right onto Hide and Seek.

9.1 Take the Hide and Seek cutoff to Homestead Road.

9.2 Turn left onto Homestead Road.

9.9 Turn right onto Flow Motion.

Sandy Ridge

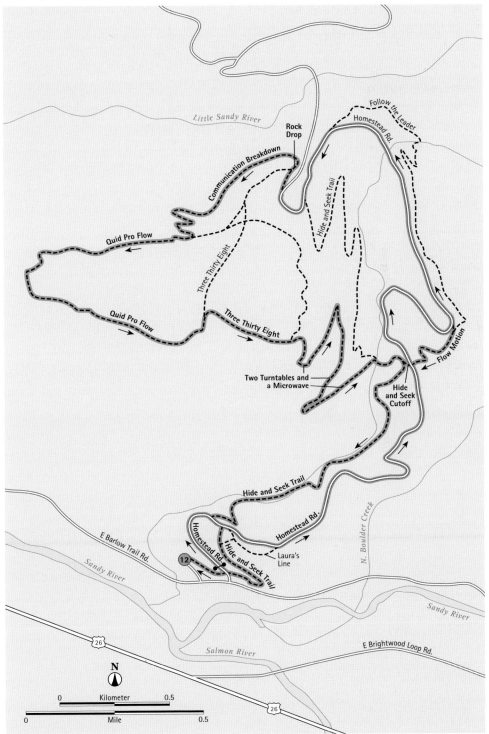

10.5   Take the cutoff to Hide and Seek.

10.6   Turn left onto Hide and Seek Trail.

12.6   Arrive back at the trailhead.

Local Information

....

Post-pedal food and drink: Calamity Jane's, 42015 SE US 26, Sandy

Adventure 13: Syncline

Finding your way around the Syncline/Coyote Wall can be a bit of a struggle. There are unmarked or unofficial trails everywhere. But it's a great ride. And the views from the heart of the Columbia River Gorge are spectacular. The geological feature known as the Syncline, though in this case a bit of a misnomer, is in the transition zone of Washington. This is where the flora, fauna, and weather begin a dramatic change from the rainy conditions of the west to the arid environs of the east. Because of this, the Syncline is a great place to go riding when things are still wet and cold in Portland.

Start: Syncline Trailhead

Distance: 4.0-mile lollipop

Riding time: 1 to 3 hours

Difficulty rating: Intermediate to difficult

Trail surface: Singletrack, doubletrack, dirt roads

Elevation gain: Up to 2,500 feet; 800 feet as described in this ride

Land status: National scenic area

Seasons: Late winter to fall

Nearest town: Bingen, Washington

Other trail users: Hikers; equestrians May to Nov

Canine compatibility: Leashed dogs permitted

Wheels: Suspension recommended

Fees and permits: Toll bridge

Restrooms: Vault toilet at the trailhead

Maps: *DeLorme: Washington Atlas & Gazetteer:* Page 101 C9

Special considerations: Rattlesnakes, poison oak, and ticks become an issue in late spring and summer.

Getting there: From Portland, take I-84 East to exit 64. Cross the toll bridge into Washington and make a right onto WA 14. Go through Bingen and continue 2 miles past town to Courtney Road. Turn left onto Courtney; trailhead parking is on the left. Cross the street and ride along Old Highway 8 for 0.5 mile to the access to the trail system, on the left. GPS: N45° 42.027' / W121° 24.153'

The Ride

Starting out along an abandoned segment of Old Highway 8, keep an eye out for an access trail about 0.6 mile from the start of the road. Follow this singletrack path upward. After one big, sweeping turn, the path widens and becomes a jeep road. The Little Maui Trail continues sharply to the right and is more fun to come down than go up. So stay straight and continue up the jeep road, passing a junction with the Little Moab Trail. After about 2 miles of riding, you'll come to another junction with the Little Maui Trail. Peel off to the right and follow Little Maui as the trail levels out. Take in the sweeping views now, because once the downhill starts, you'll want your faculties about you. There are plenty of spots for speed here, but corners can be tight and there are a few loose areas, so use the speed judiciously. Follow the trail all the way back down to Old Highway 8 and back to the trailhead to complete the 4.0-mile loop.

Alternatively, you can follow the jeep road up to the face of Coyote Wall and a junction with the Little Moab Trail. This is an exciting run along a rather sheer cliff back down to Old Highway 8. Read that last sentence again. This is *not* a trail for the faint of heart or the unsure. The penalty for failure along the Little Moab Trail is severe indeed. And it's happened in the past. So please exercise extreme caution if this is your chosen route down.

The Little Moab Trail skirts along the edge of the Syncline.

Syncline

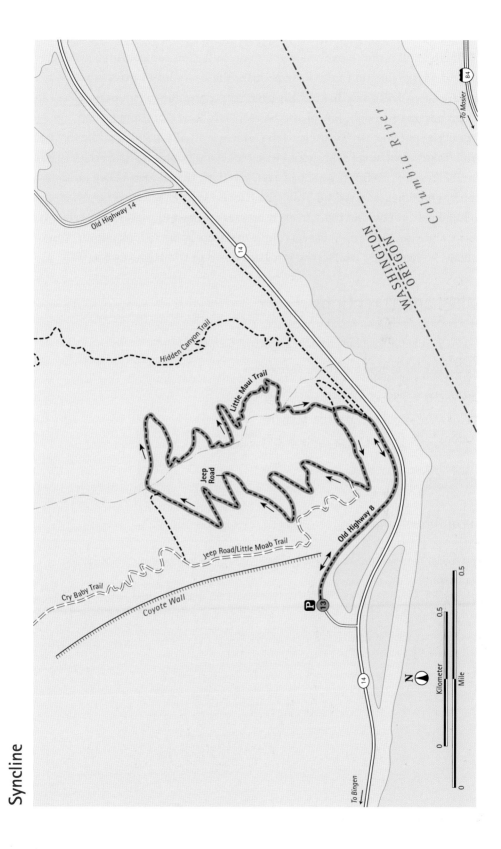

There's still more to explore if you're up to it. You can continue up the jeep road to a large junction near a farmhouse. There is a lot of private property in this area. Residents have historically been very amenable to mountain bikers and hikers passing through, but please be respectful and obey any posted signage. From this spot you can continue to the west, eventually arriving at the Cry Baby Trail. Take everything I said about Little Moab and double it. That's the Cry Baby Trail. Please be careful. If you head east, you'll hit the Hidden Valley (or Canyon as it's sometimes referred to) Trail. The Hidden Valley Trail traverses wide-open rolling fields, rocks, and tight trees. It crosses creeks and passes a waterfall. It is an absolute joy, but it does have a couple exposure spots to look out for. You can follow Hidden Valley Trail all the way back down to Old Highway 8 as well.

Miles and Directions

0.0   Start at the trailhead and ride east on Old Highway 8.

0.5   Take the path on the left and follow it up.

0.8   Stay straight on the jeep road at a junction.

2.2   Make a right onto the Little Maui Trail.

3.5   Arrive back at Old Highway 8. Make a right.

4.0   Arrive back at the trailhead.

Local Information

Post-pedal food and drink: Everybody's Brewing, 151 W Jewett Blvd., White Salmon, Washington

Adventure 14: Ape Canyon to Plains of Abraham

The Northwest is renowned for the diversity of its landscape. The entire region is a geological grab bag, thanks in large part to its volcanic history. Some of the most dramatic diversity can be found near the volcanoes responsible for the lay of the land. The Mount St. Helens eruption of 1980 left a great amount of destruction in its wake. But almost thirty-five years later, the landscape has recovered more quickly than anyone could have imagined. Though the blast zone still resembles a lunar landscape, life has returned to the area, and the region continues to morph noticeably from season to season.

Some of the best singletrack within extended driving distance of Portland, the ride along the Ape Canyon Trail to the Plains of Abraham starts out in pristine forest but soon delivers you to the Mount St. Helens blast zone. A classic out-and-back day ride starts at the Ape Canyon Trailhead and ascends to the Windy Ridge Viewpoint. If you're really adventurous and enjoy unpredictability, a loop descending the Smith Creek Trail should satiate that hunger nicely.

Start: Ape Canyon Trailhead

Distance: 19.2 miles out and back (22.2-mile loop option)

Riding time: 2.5 to 4 hours

Difficulty rating: Intermediate to difficult

Trail surface: Singletrack, gravel road

Elevation gain: 2,600 feet

Land status: National forest

Seasons: Summer

Nearest town: Cougar, Washington

Other trail users: Hikers

Canine compatibility: Leashed dogs permitted but not recommended

Wheels: Suspension recommended

Fees and permits: Northwest Forest Pass or day-use fee

Restrooms: At Windy Ridge Viewpoint parking area

Maps: *DeLorme: Washington Atlas & Gazetteer*: Page 88 D2

Special considerations: Snow can cover trail segments into late June. Weather gets nasty and unpredictable by the time October rolls around. Check conditions before you go. Once you're out of the forest and onto the plains, it's 100 percent exposure. Bring your sunscreen and lots of water.

Getting there: From Portland, take I-5 North to WA 503 toward Cougar. Make a left onto FR 83 toward the Ape Canyon Trailhead. Drive 11.5 more miles and make a left into the Ape Canyon Trailhead parking lot. GPS: N46° 9.921' / W122° 5.527'

The Ride

From the trailhead the ride begins in young forest before entering imposing stands of Douglas, noble, and silver firs. The climbing is steady here, with a handful of switchbacks thrown into the mix. The trail is typical Northwest forest singletrack at this point—some roots, some rocks. Nothing overly technical here, just steady climbing through scenic forest. Toward the top of the climb things open up, with views of Ape Canyon, Mount St. Helens, and Mount Adams on clear days.

You're now in the blast zone, and it's obvious. Now on the Loowit Trail, it looks and feels as though you're biking on the moon. The change is a little breathtaking. In the distance trees strewn like matchsticks cling to hillsides and snags dot the landscape. Still standing in place, the snags are ghostly reminders of

Spirit Lake peeks from around the corner.

THE MOSIER SYNCLINE

If you've ever spent much time exploring the eastern Columbia River Gorge, you may have heard of the Mosier Syncline, which descends from the Washington side of the Columbia River across from the Oregon town of Mosier. However, calling it a syncline is a bit of a misnomer. At Mosier the true syncline forms the channel for the Columbia River and then turns from an east–west orientation and heads off to the southwest in the direction of Mount Hood. The exposed scarp on the Washington side of the Gorge is actually a highly visible part of one of the limbs of the syncline-anticline structure and not the syncline itself. Hikers and mountain bikers know it as Coyote Wall.

The Mosier Syncline is a popular hiking and mountain-biking destination on the Washington side of the Columbia River Gorge.

the three-decades-old devastation. The riding is mostly flat and wide open here. Views abound, but this is a pumice field. The trail can be loose, and there are some washouts to negotiate.

The Mount St. Helens crater looms in the background from a trail junction.

After almost 6 miles of riding, you'll turn onto the Abraham Trail and cruise through the Plains of Abraham. The trail is a lot of fun here, with easy rolling elevation changes. The path weaves its way along a ridge, offering up incredible views of Mount St. Helens. The crater is on full display here, as is Spirit Lake. The Abraham Trail spits out onto FR 99 and quickly delivers you to the Windy Ridge Viewpoint parking area. There are restrooms and some more great views to take in. To complete the ride, head back the way you came.

Option: For an epic but technical and unpredictable loop, continue onto the Smith Creek Trail. Also scenic, the trail is fast and loose, alternating between single- and doubletrack. The trail is subject to washouts, can be easy to lose in some places, and requires water crossings. Research this one before attempting it, and, if you can, go with someone who has done it.

Miles and Directions

0.0   Start from the parking area and begin up the Ape Canyon Trail.

Ape Canyon to Plains of Abraham

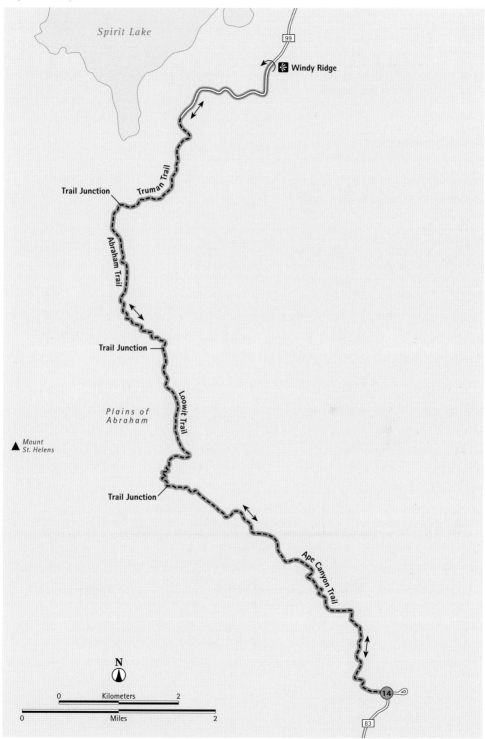

Spirit Lake

99

Windy Ridge

Truman Trail

Trail Junction

Abraham Trail

Trail Junction

Loowit Trail

Plains of Abraham

Mount St. Helens

Trail Junction

Ape Canyon Trail

14

83

N

0   Kilometers   2

0   Miles   2

4.1	Make a slight right onto the Loowit Trail.
5.8	Turn right onto Abraham Trail (216D).
8.0	Turn right onto the Truman Trail (207).
9.6	Arrive at Windy Ridge Viewpoint. Head back the way you came.
19.2	Arrive back at the trailhead.

Local Information

Post-pedal food and drink: In Cougar, check out Cougar Bar & Grill, 16849 Lewis River Rd., or Lone Fir Cafe, 16806 Lewis River Rd.

HIKING

Hiking was my gateway drug into the outdoors. And if I'm being honest, it's still probably my favorite activity. There are countless miles of hiking trails within the city of Portland alone. Forest Park boasts more than 80 miles of hiking trails, and that's just one park! In Portland you can hike (or paddle) around both the largest protected wetland and largest forested natural area in an American city. Get out of town and things ramp up exponentially. The Columbia River Gorge, the country's first national scenic area, is home to some of the nation's best hiking. You can visit lush rain forests, Technicolor wildflower meadows, wide-open prairies, vista-laden summits, deep canyons, etc., etc., etc.—all in the immediate vicinity. Here's some suggestions for hiking in the city and beyond.

The upper meadows of Dog Mountain come into bloom.

Recommended Outfitters and Guide Services

Next Adventure. Everything you need for hiking, backpacking, and beyond. Tons of new and used gear; their Bargain Basement has the best deals on close-outs and recycled gear in the city (nextadventure.net).

REI. Advice, classes, guided trips, and, of course, gear. REI is the standard-bearer (rei.com/stores/portland.html).

KEEN Footwear. Yes, I'm an ambassador for the company. But a big reason is because this Portland-based company handles business with the greater good in mind. And I love their shoes and boots (keenfootwear.com).

Adventure 15: Balch Creek to Pittock Mansion

Balch Creek Canyon is one of the most beautiful urban canyons to be found anywhere. The transition from crowded city streets to peaceful canopied trail and flourishing canyon happens so quickly that you'll find it hard to believe a bustling city is just steps away. Located in the Macleay Park section of Forest Park, the trail begins at the Lower Macleay Park Trailhead and soon joins up with the Wildwood Trail. From there the possibilities are endless. The time-tested route up to the Pittock Mansion is just one of a number of classic outings in this area.

Distance: 5.2 miles out and back

Elevation gain: 850 feet

Difficulty: Moderate

Trail surface: Hard-packed dirt; duffy, rocky

Hiking time: 1.5 to 3 hours

County: Clark

Land status: City park

Seasons: All

Fees and permits: None for park or mansion grounds; fee to enter mansion

Restrooms: At Audubon Society and Pittock Mansion

Trail contact: City of Portland, Parks & Recreation, (503) 823-6007; portland oregon.gov/parks/

Maps: *Oregon Road & Recreation Atlas*: Page 106 D4

Finding the trailhead: From I-405 in downtown Portland, take exit 3 for US 30 toward St. Helens. Immediately exit onto NW Vaughn Street and drive 0.3 mile to NW 26th Street. Turn left and then make an almost immediate right onto NW Upshur Street. Follow Upshur for 0.5 mile to the parking area at the end of the street. Find the path by walking under the suspension bridge. The park will funnel you toward the trail. GPS: N 45° 32.156' / W 122° 42.742'

The Hike

Leaving from the lower trailhead at the terminus of Northwest Upshur Street, the trail begins smooth and paved as it enters the canyon. But the concrete soon ends, and the surroundings become more wild and lush as the canyon walls rise.

Exploring the grounds of the Pittock Mansion

The largest Douglas fir trees in Portland are in this part of the park, as well as native cutthroat trout. Discovered in 1987, the small population of trout that reside in the creek helped solidify efforts to restore the health of the entire watershed.

After 0.8 mile you'll come to a junction with the Wildwood Trail. Just past this turnoff you'll find the Stone House, also known as the "Witch's Castle." Despite its medieval appearance, what remains here is the stone framework of an elaborate rest station, once with bathrooms, that was originally erected by the Civilian Conservation Corps back in the 1930s.

Continue straight along the path that follows the creek and cross over a footbridge. Soon the trail ascends three long switchbacks to Upper Macleay Park. If you're interested, the Audubon Society of Portland is just 100 yards or so to the right. There's a bird sanctuary, a gift shop, and restrooms if needed. To continue the hike, stay on the Wildwood Trail as it bends around the parking lot; use the crosswalk to cross Cornell Road and pick up the path on the other side. The trail continues steadily uphill through some very scenic woods to the Pittock Mansion parking lot. Stay on the Wildwood Trail at all junctions.

FOREST PARK

Most city parks are essentially islands of green space surrounded by concrete. As a result, most of the wildlife that once occupied that space flees or perishes—leaving the park dominated by pigeons and squirrels. Forest Park is different. The park is bordered on one side by Portland, but on the other side the Tualatin Mountains extend all the way to the Oregon Coast Range. And because there is limited development, the Tualatin Mountains are home to an uninterrupted nature corridor, allowing wildlife to come in and out of Forest Park as it pleases. As a result, more than fifty species of mammals inhabit the park, including black-tailed deer, black bear, and elk. More than one hundred species of birds can also be found here, including bald eagle and peregrine falcon, which can occasionally be seen patrolling the skies over Portland.

Hiking along Forest Park's Wildwood Trail

Hiking alongside Balch Creek

From the parking lot walk downhill to the left, toward the mansion. You're free to explore the grounds at no charge, but there is a fee to go inside. Walk past the restrooms and through the open lawn area, down to a viewpoint of the city. On a clear day the whole metropolis is on display from this vantage, as are a handful of Cascade peaks. Head back the way you came.

Miles and Directions

0.0 From the trailhead, walk under the bridge along a paved path that parallels Balch Creek. The path eventually becomes unpaved trail.

0.8 Come to the Witch's Castle and a junction with the Wildwood Trail. Continue straight.

1.4 Arrive at a parking area and Cornell Road. Use the crosswalk to carefully cross the road and pick up the trail on the other side. Stay on the Wildwood Trail at all junctions.

2.4 Reach the Pittock Mansion parking lot. Walk down to the viewpoint.

Balch Creek to Pittock Mansion

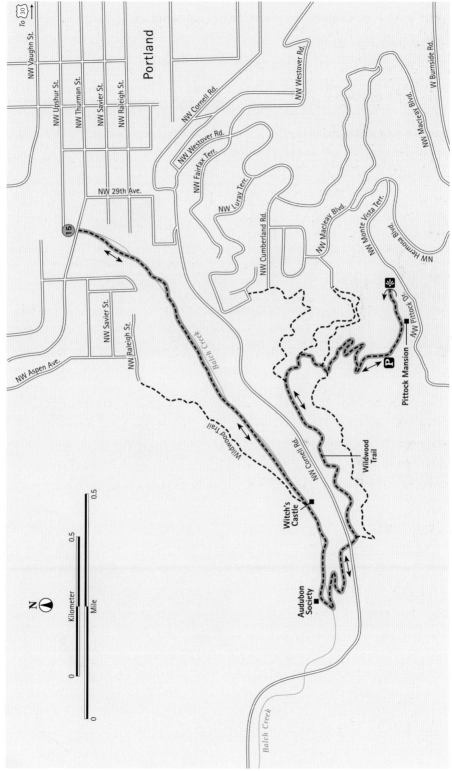

2.6 Arrive at the viewpoint. Head back the way you came.

5.2 Arrive back at the trailhead.

Local Information

Post-hike food and drink: In Portland, check out Rae's Lakeview Lounge, 1900 NW 27th Ave., or Industrial Cafe and Saloon, 2572 NW Vaughn St.

Adventure 16: 4T Trail

A number of assets place Portland near the top of the list of America's most-livable cities. Among them, public transportation, green spaces, and a walkable downtown area all contribute mightily. If you are in town for one day and want to soak up as much as you can of the good stuff this place has to offer, the 4T Trail should be somewhere near the top of your list.

The *T*'s of the 4T Trail stand for Trail, Tram, Trolley (Portland streetcar), and Train (MAX). When combined, these *T*'s create an approximately 9-mile loop and a quintessential Portland experience. The 4T highlights urban parks and trails, stunning views of volcanoes and cityscapes, a tram ride, and our legendary public transportation.

Signage along the route is pretty good, and you might only need to occasionally glance at a map to track your progress. There are four different trailheads, one for each T of the trip: where tram meets trolley at the South Waterfront, where tram meets trail at Oregon Health & Science University (OHSU), where trail meets train at the Oregon Zoo, and where train meets trolley at the downtown library. This is great, because you can tailor your adventure accordingly. Depending on what time of day you set off, you may want to begin and end downtown for lunch or happy hour.

Distance: 4.1 miles of hiking; 9.0 miles total

Difficulty: Easy

Trail surface: Hard-packed dirt; duffy, rocky

Hiking time: 1.5 to 3 hours

County: Multnomah

Land status: City, city park, hospital

Seasons: All

Fees and permits: Fees for public transit

Restrooms: At OHSU, various locations downtown

Trail contact: The 4T, 4ttrail.wordpress.com

Maps: *Oregon Road & Recreation Atlas:* Page 106 D4

Finding the trailhead: You can start pretty much anywhere along the route. A recommended start is downtown, one stop west of Pioneer Courthouse Square at the Galleria/SW 10th Avenue stop. GPS: N45° 31.188' / W122° 40.897'

The Hike

Begin downtown at the Central Library with the "Train" segment of the loop. Head to the westbound MAX stop at 10th and Morrison, buy yourself a day pass, and hop on the next train. At 260 feet below the surface, the MAX station at Washington Park is the deepest transit station in North America! Get off here and take the elevator up to the zoo parking area.

Now you get to enjoy a little trail time with a 4.1-mile hike over to OHSU. From the Washington Park MAX station, walk over to the zoo and head downhill along the sidewalk. Keep an eye out for 4T signage. You'll encounter these helpful little signs all along the route, and always at critical trail junctions. Cross over US 26 and make a left, heading downhill. Be careful crossing here, and don't take the unmarked bootpath that you'll encounter first. Look for the marked Marquam Trail. Admittedly, this first section of trail isn't all that scenic, and it takes awhile to get away from the traffic noise. But it gets you out of the city and into the trees pretty quickly, as a good trail should. After a handful of miles and some road crossings, you'll arrive at Council Crest, the highest point in Portland proper. Believe it or not, they once crammed an amusement park on this

The view of Portland from the OHSU tram

PUBLIC TRANSPORTATION

Part of the "Downtown Plan" that was conceived and implemented in the 1970s and '80s was a major push for public transportation improvements. As a result, the City of Portland has one of the best and most user-friendly public transportation programs in America. It may not be the gratis "Fareless Square" it was a few years ago, but it's still relatively inexpensive and gets you pretty much anywhere you want to be.

With a handful of outlying exceptions, you can get to many of the adventure in this book by utilizing public transit. You can take bikes on MAX trains and streetcars, and buses have racks for them. If you're new to the area or just new to public transportation in Portland, a great way to get your feet wet is Adventure 16, the 4T Trail. In one outing you'll get a taste of everything except a bus. And you can always take that to get downtown. Trimet.org has all the public transit information you'll need; a wonderful blog, portlandby bus.com, covers a wide variety of amazing things you can do in this city via public transit, including restaurants on the route and hiking trails.

elevated plot of land complete with roller coaster. Soak up the views and take a well-earned breather before descending into the Marquam Nature Park. The hike now becomes decidedly more scenic, with stately Douglas firs and western red cedar lining the path. Now you're going to lose a lot of the elevation you just gained, only to claim it back with a climb up to OHSU.

The next segment is the "Tram" at OHSU. Hours vary, but the ride is free since you're heading down. The journey is brief but breathtaking. If it's a clear day, have your camera ready, as you'll get good views of Mounts Hood and St. Helens. Once you exit the tram, the OHSU Commons Streetcar (trolley) stop is just steps away.

The streetcar signifies the end of hiking or standing, so take a load off. Enjoy the ride, and take in the new construction and the hubbub of the burgeoning South Waterfront. Exit at the Central Library and you've completed the 4T Trail.

Thanks to the fact that the 4T Trail makes a giant loop through the heart of downtown Portland, it provides the opportunity to explore along the route. And I would encourage you to do so. Roam around Washington Park while you're up at the zoo. Get off anywhere during your trolley ride and walk along the South Waterfront. And then, of course, there is downtown. The place where this little

The MAX stop at Washington Park

adventure begins and ends is home to "Portland's Living Room"—Pioneer Court-house Square, the Pioneer Place Mall, food carts, etc. Take your time and enjoy them. Portland's a great place to live. And the 4T Trail does a bang up job of showing you why.

Miles and Directions

0.0   Start from the Washington Park MAX stop and walk toward the zoo and downhill toward US 26; cross over the highway on a bridge.

0.5   Reach the Marquam Trail. Continue hiking.

1.1   Cross SW Humphrey Boulevard. Follow signage for the 4T Trail.

1.7   Arrive at Council Crest. Walk down the east side of Council Crest to continue on the Marquam Trail.

2.8   At a junction, stay right to continue on the Marquam Trail.

3.0   Come to a junction with the Shelter Loop Trail. Make a hard left onto the Shelter Loop Trail.

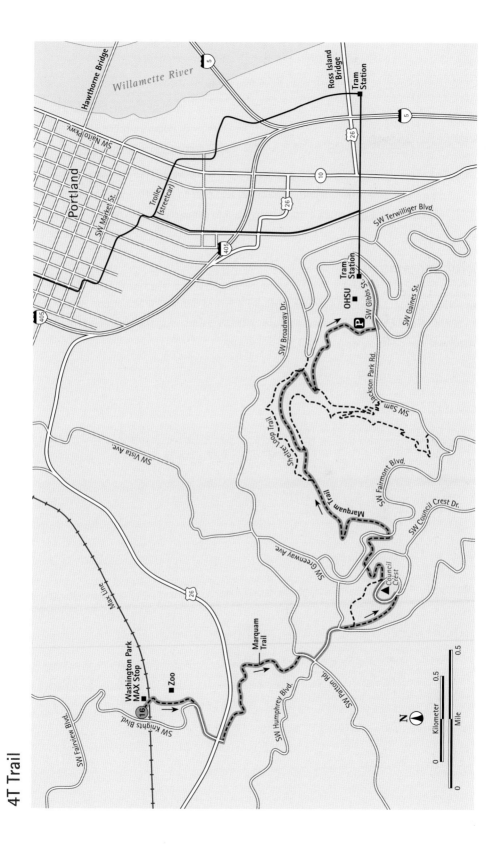

3.4 Arrive at the Marquam Shelter and make a right at a junction, heading uphill.

3.5 At the junction, make a left onto the Connor Trail.

3.9 Come to a parking lot. Walk down SW 9th Street to SW Gibbs Street. Make a left onto SW Gibbs. Continue downhill past the Emergency Room entrance. Under the second pedestrian bridge, there is a set of stairs entering the hospital.

4.1 Take these stairs, enter the hospital building, and follow signs to the tram. At the South Waterfront Tram Terminal, walk 100 feet over to the OHSU Commons Streetcar stop. Take this to the Central Library Stop to complete the 4T Trail.

Local Information

Post-hike food and drink: Downtown Portland = lots of options. Solid options include the 9th & Alder Food Cart Pod; The Picnic House, 723 SW Salmon St.; the Imperial, 410 SW Broadway; and Bailey's Taproom, 213 SW Broadway.

Adventure 17: Hoyt Arboretum

Located in Portland's Washington Park, the Hoyt Arboretum is home to more than 2,000 species of trees and plants from all over the world. Far more than just a simple walk through a living museum of trees, there are 12 miles of hiking trails spread out over 189 acres. The paths wind through groups of trees including larch, spruce, oak, and even sequoia. There is no charge to visit the arboretum, which features a visitor center staffed with highly knowledgeable volunteers. There is a research library, as well as an assortment of free maps and brochures.

The arboretum is gorgeous. It's also a labyrinth. To be honest, the odds of getting through a hike in this place for the first time without making a quizzical look at a trail junction are slim, even with a map. But the signage is excellent. and it would be difficult to become truly lost. Worst case scenario is that you accidentally add an extra mile or two to your outing.

Distance: 3.2-mile loop

Difficulty: Easy

Trail surface: Hard-packed dirt, duffy, rocky, paved

Hiking time: 1.5 to 3 hours

County: Multnomah

Land status: City park

Seasons: All

Fees and permits: Parking fee

Restrooms: At the arboretum visitor center

Trail contact: City of Portland, Parks & Recreation, (503) 823-6007; portland oregon.gov/parks/

Maps: *Oregon Road & Recreation Atlas:* Page 106 D4

Finding the trailhead: From downtown Portland, take US 26 West to exit 72 for the Oregon Zoo. Stay right and drive up past the Children's Museum and World Forestry Center. Continue to a small parking area on the right, just before an intersection with SW Kingston Drive. GPS: N45° 30.769' / W122° 42.999'

The Hike

If you're not able to find a spot in the small lot, which is a possibility, you can park in the main parking area you passed on the way in. There's an hourly fee no matter where you park, so no need to be overly picky. Make your way to the

Marquam Trail and up to the Wildwood. There are a number of user paths that mimic official trails here, but they're all heading in essentially the same direction. This area is chock-full of trilliums in spring. After a road crossing, you'll continue onto the White Pine Trail.

The path is mostly level, scenic, and relatively secluded. Keep an eye out for helpfully labeled flora throughout the hike. As you would suspect, trail names tend to coincide with the sort of trees you're hiking through. After taking in the pines, make a road crossing and pick up the Wildwood Trail. You'll hike just into the fringe of the redwood area, highlighted by the glorious perch that is the redwood observation deck.

Continuing down the Fir Trail, cross another road and stop in at the visitor center. There are restrooms here and a metric ton of information about the arboretum and more. The hike now follows a path down through a grove of oaks and over to the Winter Garden and the Magnolia Trail. There are some places in Portland you need to be at certain times of the year. The Magnolia Trail in springtime is one of them. A stroll along this path on the right day will take your breath away.

Visitors enjoying the Magnolia Trail in bloom

Looking up at redwoods in the Hoyt Arboretum

The trail ascends a very photogenic set of switchbacks, crosses yet another road, and crests at a water tank. Rejoining the Wildwood, the trail passes a number of interesting nonnative species as it descends back to the parking area and the end of the hike. Almost anywhere you hike in Portland is going to showcase something different depending on what time of year you visit. No place is better at that than the Hoyt Arboretum.

Miles and Directions

0.0 Start from the parking area and carefully cross SW Knights Boulevard at a crosswalk. Pick up the Marquam Trail and follow it to the Wildwood Trail after about 400 feet. Make a left onto the Wildwood.

0.2 Take a connector trail on the left that ascends and crosses SW Fairview Boulevard. Hike up the White Pine Trail. Stay on this trail, passing a number of junctions.

1.0 Arrive at SW Fischer Lane. Carefully cross the road and pick up the connector trail on the other side. Follow this down to a junction with the Wildwood Trail and make a right. Stay on the Wildwood Trail at all junctions.

Hoyt Arboretum

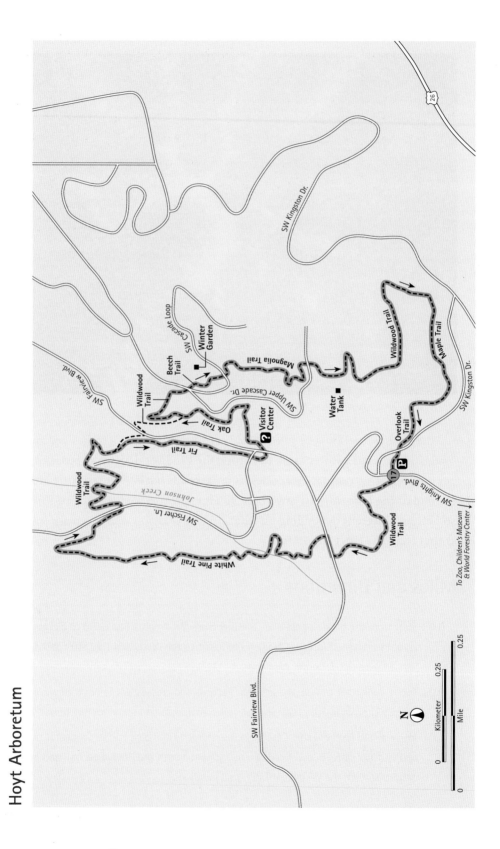

1.4 Pass the first junction with the Fir Trail. Arrive at a second and follow this south, paralleling the road to the left.

1.6 Just before reaching a pavilion on the right, take the connector trail on the left, crossing SW Fairview Boulevard and arriving at the visitor center. On the northwest side of the visitor center, pick up the Oak Trail, staying on this trail at all junctions.

1.9 The Oak Trail terminates at a junction with the Wildwood Trail. Make a right and stay on the Wildwood Trail as it descends to a double road crossing of SW Upper Cascade Drive and SW Cascade Loop. Pick up the Wildwood Trail on the other side.

2.1 Arrive at a junction and make a right onto the Beech Trail. Walk through the Winter Garden and follow the Magnolia Trail on an ascending set of switchbacks to a road crossing.

2.2 Cross SW Upper Cascade Drive and pick up the Magnolia Trail. At a junction with the Wildwood Trail, make a left.

2.6 Make a left to stay on the Wildwood Trail.

2.8 Pass a junction with the Walnut Trail. Arrive at a junction and make a right onto the Maple Trail.

3.1 Stay left at a junction with the Overlook Trail. Cross SW Kingston Drive.

3.2 Arrive back at the parking area.

Local Information

Post-hike food and drink: Come back down the hill to the Goose Hollow Inn, 1927 SW Jefferson St.

Adventure 18: North Wildwood Trail

Without a doubt, Forest Park's Wildwood Trail is the preeminent hiking path in the city of Portland. It is the most well-known trail in the most well-known park in town. If you hike in Portland, you've been on this trail—and more than likely run into several fellow outdoor lovers in the process.

But remember, the Wildwood Trail stretches the length of Forest Park, the largest forested municipal park in the country. That's just over 30 miles of potential hiking that can be done on the Wildwood alone. So have you been to the end? Not where the trail "begins" in Washington Park but where it ends, off US 30 in Linnton.

Distance: 3.4 miles out and back

Difficulty: Easy

Trail surface: Hard-packed dirt; duffy, rocky

Hiking time: 1.5 to 3 hours

County: Multnomah

Land status: City park

Seasons: All

Trail contact: City of Portland, Parks & Recreation, (503) 823-6007; portland oregon.gov/parks/

Maps: *Oregon Road & Recreation Atlas*: Page 106 B2

Finding the trailhead: From downtown Portland, take I-405 North to US 30. Take US 30 to St. Helens for just over 8 miles and make a left onto Newberry Road. At 1.5 miles, look for a small pullout at the trailhead, on the left. GPS: N45° 36.314' / W122° 49.456'

The Hike

There are a few good reasons to visit this area of the park. For starters it's far less crowded. Also, and perhaps even more important, this section of the Wildwood features only native flora. There are no invasive species (e.g., English ivy) to be found along this segment of the trail. Combine these factors and you also get the happy by-product of more wildlife. An easy 3.4-mile out-and-back hike from the end of the Wildwood Trail is a great introduction to Forest Park's wilder side.

From the trailhead the Wildwood Trail immediately descends to a bridged creek crossing, ascending again on the other side. The entire length of the

Wildwood follows a pattern of easy, rolling elevation gains and losses paired with winding canyon explorations. Along the way the trail passes through shady stands of western red cedar engulfed by carpets of oxalis, stately groves of Douglas fir and hemlock, and expanses of gnarled, moss-covered maples. You'll encounter all of the aforementioned on this hike. This area is also a hotbed for trilliums in spring.

Continuing, the trail crosses several bridges dripping with mosses and lichens in the wet season. After ducking in and out of a few canyons, things open up a bit and the path bends easily through the forest. A brief climb reaches an opening under a set of power lines before ducking back into a canyon and arriving at Fire Lane 15, the turnaround point for this hike. If you're in the mood for more, continue as long as you like before returning the way you came.

Miles and Directions

0.0 Start at the trailhead and proceed onto the signed Wildwood Trail.

1.5 Continue hiking beneath a set of power lines.

Hiking along the Wildwood Trail on the north end of the park

North Wildwood Trail

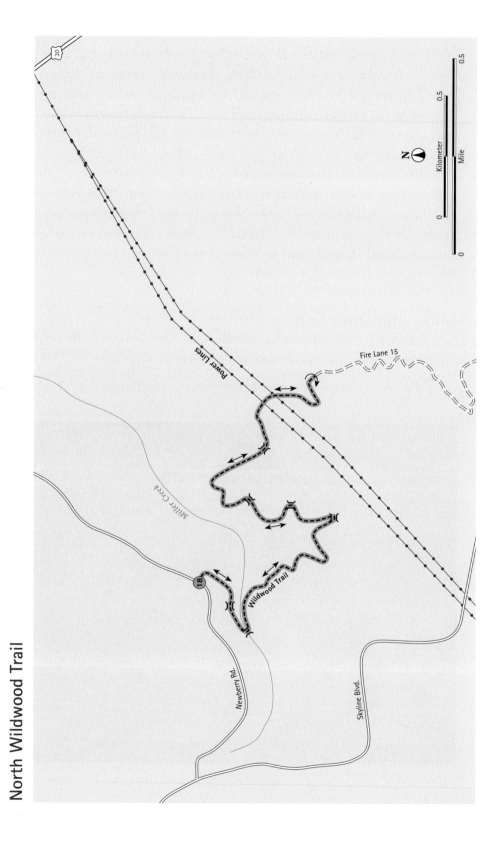

A small creek crossing along the Wildwood Trail

1.7 Arrive at a junction with Fire Lane 15. Head back the way you came.

3.4 Arrive back at the trailhead.

Local Information

Post-hike food and drink: Head into the St. Johns neighborhood and visit the Leisure Public House, 8002 N Lombard St., or the Taqueria in the back of Tienda Santa Cruz, 8630 N Lombard St.

Adventure 19: Tryon Creek State Park

Tryon Creek State Park is one of the more well-known outdoor spots in Portland. The 658-acre natural area is Oregon's only state park within a major metropolitan area. Thanks in large part to Friends of Tryon Creek, there are a number of attractions and activities that make the park one of the city's more popular destinations, including 8 miles of hiking trails, 3.5 miles of horse trails, 3 miles of paved bike paths, and a nature center. The park also offers guided hikes, summer day camps, junior ranger programs, and a litany of special events. A 2.1-mile loop around the grounds is a great way to get a feel for what the park has to offer.

Distance: 2.1-mile loop

Difficulty: Easy

Trail surface: Hard-packed dirt; rocky, paved

Hiking time: 0.5 to 3 hours

County: Multnomah

Land status: State park

Seasons: All

Restrooms: At the nature center

Trail contact: City of Portland, Parks & Recreation, (503) 823-6007; portland oregon.gov/parks/

Maps: *Oregon Road & Recreation Atlas:* Page 106 F4

Finding the trailhead: From downtown Portland, take I-5 South to exit 297. Head south on Terwilliger Boulevard, following signs for Tryon Creek State Park. After just over 2 miles, turn right onto the entrance road and follow it to the parking area. Maps of the park's trails are provided inside the nature center. GPS: N45° 26.488' / W122° 40.559'

The Hike

From the nature center, head south along the paved Old Main Trail. Pass a junction with the Big Fir Trail on the right and continue to a junction with the Red Fox Trail. Take the slight left onto the Red Fox Trail and descend on the dirt path to a bridge that crosses Tryon Creek. Pass a junction with the South Creek Trail and continue to a junction with the Cedar Trail. Douglas fir, red alder, big-leaf maple, vine maple, cottonwood, hemlock, and western red cedar trees can

The Old Main Trail at Tryon Creek

be found throughout the park. And while the first 0.5 mile was dominated by maples and cottonwoods, the next 0.5 mile ascends through a shady grove of cedars.

After 1 mile of total hiking, pass a junction with the Hemlock Trail on the left; continue on the Cedar Trail. The path rolls and weaves through the park now, occasionally climbing and diving into and over ridges. The trail soon arrives at the Bunk Bridge and crosses over quietly babbling Park Creek. Stay straight at a junction with the West Horse Loop and arrive at a potentially confusing trail junction with another horse trail. Stay straight and immediately encounter another junction with the Middle Creek Trail. Make a left here and follow the path as it parallels Tryon Creek.

Cross another bridge and make an immediate right to stay on the Middle Creek Trail. At a junction the Middle Creek Trail takes a right turn. Stay straight here, now on the Maple Ridge Trail. A short distance later, at another junction, make a right and arrive back at the nature center and main parking area.

Tryon Creek State Park

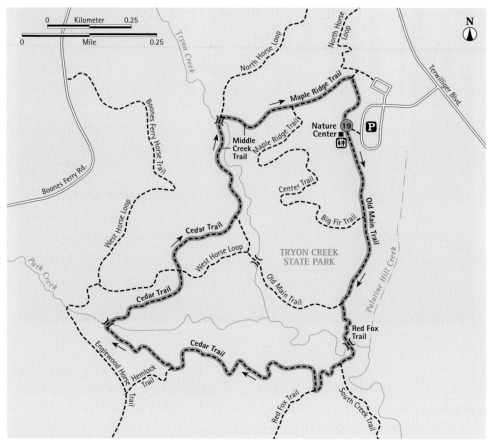

Miles and Directions

0.0 Start from the nature center and head south on the paved Old Main Trail.

0.1 Stay straight at a junction with the Big Fir Trail.

0.3 Make a slight left onto the Red Fox Trail.

0.6 Make a right onto the Cedar Trail.

1.0 Stay right at a junction with the Hemlock Trail.

1.4 Stay straight at a junction with the West Horse Loop.

1.6 Stay straight at a junction with a horse trail.

1.7 Arrive at a junction with the Middle Creek Trail and make a left.

1.8 Turn right to stay on the Middle Creek Trail.

1.9 Stay straight and continue onto the Maple Ridge Trail.

2.1 Make a right to return to the nature center and main parking area.

Local Information

Post-hike food and drink: Oswego Grill, 7 Centerpointe Dr., Lake Oswego

Adventure 20: Powell Butte

Powell Butte is just one in a series of extinct volcanic mounds that form the Boring/East Buttes Lava Domes. This range contains some of the largest contiguous wildlife habitats in the area. The 600-acre Powell Butte Nature Park provides over 9 miles of trails for hikers, mountain bikers, and horseback riders. There is also a 0.5-mile barrier-free trail leading to the top of the butte, where views of Mount St. Helens and Mount Hood dominate the horizon.

Grassland meadows, a scrub shrub transition area, and a mid–seral stage forest all provide home to a wide array of wildlife. This diverse habitat also affords hikers the opportunity to catch a glimpse of one of the many birds, mammals, and reptiles that make the butte home.

Distance: 3.7-mile loop

Difficulty: Easy

Trail surface: Hard-packed dirt, gravel; duffy, rocky

Hiking time: 1.5 to 3 hours

County: Multnomah

Land status: City park

Seasons: All, though some trails close in muddier conditions

Restrooms: At the visitor center

Trail contact: City of Portland, Parks & Recreation, (503) 823-6007; portland oregon.gov/parks/

Maps: *Oregon Road & Recreation Atlas:* Page 107 E7

Finding the trailhead: From I-205, take exit 19 and head east on Powell for 3.5 miles. Turn right onto 162nd Avenue and drive up to the main parking area near the restrooms. GPS: N45° 29.424' / W122° 29.836'

The Hike

There's an awful lot to explore here, but this 3.7-mile loop will give you a pretty good sampling. Most of the trails on Powell Butte are multiuse. And because the butte is home to some of Portland's best in-city singletrack, expect to encounter mountain bikers. So look alive.

For this hike start south along the paved Mountain View Trail. Things can be a little confusing in this area, with a handful of trails heading off in every direction. But the signage is good, so you'll never be in too much jeopardy. Continuing

Heading down the Cedar Grove Trail

onto the Wildhorse Trail, begin the steady but well-graded ascent to the top of Powell Butte. The summit area is wide open, with views in all directions. The best are of Mount St. Helens to the north and Mount Hood to the east. There are a couple of designated "view" spots as well if you like your vistas to be official.

After a stroll around Summit Lane, you'll descend on the Hawthorn Trail into a shady, fern-laden forest of Douglas fir and maples. As the path bends around the southwest side of the butte, the scenery gets better and the forest gets more lush. If you're not impressed yet, the Cedar Grove Trail will probably do the trick. The path begins to ascend once more, paralleling a creek lined with moisture-loving western red cedars.

After hiking along the forested west side of the butte, the climb continues along the Elderberry Trail and you reemerge into the butte's open summit space

Powell Butte

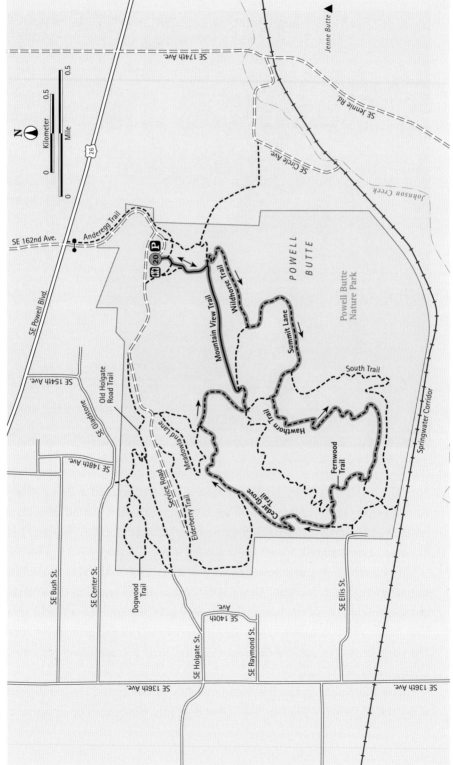

along Meadowland Lane. You'll get one more look at Cascade peaks on the Mountain View Trail before descending back to the trailhead.

Miles and Directions

0.0 Start from the visitor center and head south on the paved Mountain View Trail. Continue straight at a junction with East Access Lane and Reservoir Lane.

0.2 Arrive at a junction and proceed onto the unpaved Wildhorse Trail.

0.5 At a junction, make a left onto Summit Lane.

0.9 Continue past a junction with the South Trail.

1.0 At a junction, make a left onto the Hawthorn Trail.

1.8 At a junction, make a right onto the Fernwood Trail.

2.0 Stay straight at a junction with the Douglas Fir Trail.

2.1 Make a right onto the Cedar Grove Trail.

2.4 Make a right at a bizarre junction where the trail splits.

2.5 Continue straight as the Cedar Grove Trail joins and becomes the Elderberry Trail.

2.7 Make a slight right onto Meadowland Lane.

3.0 Make a left onto Summit Lane.

3.1 Arrive at a junction with the paved Mountain View Trail and make a left.

3.5 Arrive at a junction with the Wildhorse Trail. Stay left, toward the parking area.

3.7 Arrive back at the trailhead.

Local Information

Post-hike food and drink: McMenamins Highland Pub & Brewery, 4225 SE 182nd Ave., Gresham

Adventure 21: Lacamas Park

If you live even remotely close to the Portland metro area and you haven't paid Lacamas Park a visit, you should remedy the situation. The park has all the family-friendly trappings you would expect: barbecue/picnic areas, a playground, etc. But it's also home to Round Lake and Lacamas Creek. The hiking paths within the park visit open meadows, impressive swatches of old-growth forest, popular swimming holes, and a handful of waterfalls, including what is believed to be the only non-basalt waterfall in the Columbia River Gorge. The best wildflower show in the metro area takes place here, as does one of the area's best fall color displays. It's okay to have favorites. This is mine.

Distance: 3.2-mile lollipop

Difficulty: Easy

Trail surface: Hard-packed dirt; duffy, rocky

Hiking time: 1.5 to 3 hours

County: Clark

Land status: City park

Seasons: All

Trail contact: City of Camas, Washington, Parks & Recreation Department, (360) 834-5307; ci.camas.wa.us/index.php/parkshome

Maps: *DeLorme: Washington Atlas & Gazetteer:* Page 99 10D

Finding the trailhead: From Vancouver, Washington, head east on WA 14 to exit 12 in Camas. Stay on 6th Avenue, going straight until you reach Garfield Street. Turn left onto Garfield. Follow the WA 500 signs up the hill, veering left just before the high school and turning right at the stop sign where the highway meets Everett Street. Follow Everett for about 1 mile to a parking lot on the right, just past the light for Lake Road. Keep a sharp eye here; it's easy to miss. If you get to 35th Avenue, you've gone too far. GPS: N45° 36.236' / W122° 24.425'

The Hike

From the parking area, follow the paved path into the main park area and make your way toward Round Lake. Once you've made it to the path that parallels the lake, make a right and continue hiking. The trail passes over a dam at the base of the lake and splinters into numerous paths. Stay to the right as much as possible

The pothole formations on Lacamas Creek

here, staying close to Lacamas Creek. After 0.5 mile of total hiking, you will reach Pothole Falls.

A very popular swimming hole in summer, Pothole Falls is unique in appearance as well as composition. Water fills and swirls in small pothole-shaped pools in the bedrock, giving the falls a wide range of foot-dipping options and flow patterns depending on water levels. There are a number of dangerous bootpaths descending to the falls. If you do want to explore the area, please take care and consider some safer access points upstream. People get in trouble here with regularity. Continue hiking downstream. The path reaches some rocky outcroppings that afford the last view of the falls before turning a corner and descending steeply into attractive woods populated by western red cedar. Stay straight at a junction and follow the path as it circles around and returns to the creek.

The next section of trail is extremely attractive in autumn, when bigleaf maples line the trail with color. There are also some great spots to access the creek along this stretch. After 1.1 mile of total hiking, arrive at a bridge crossing the creek and Lower Falls. Walk out onto the bridge for views of the creek and Lower Falls. Some good views of the falls can also be had via some bootpaths

Fall hiking in Lacamas Park

just downstream from the bridge. If you continue across the bridge, you'll be treated to some very nice forest before arriving at another park access trailhead and parking area. Save that for another time.

Make a left at the bridge, following a wide gravel path. Pass a junction only 30 feet or so beyond the bridge and make a left at the second junction that appears shortly after the first. The path now ascends into the woods. After 0.2 mile stay right to remain on the main trail and hike to a T junction with a gravel road. Go left here and follow the road for 0.4 mile to an easy-to-miss junction on the left side of the gravel road. If you feel like the added exercise, take this path down into the woods. Ignore a junction and continue on the main path, eventually bending to the left and arriving at Woodburn Falls.

Nobody is going to confuse Woodburn Falls with Multnomah Falls, but the 20-foot cascade possesses its own low-flow beauty. Backtrack up to the gravel road and make a left. At the next junction make a right, heading uphill. About 300 feet later make a left at another junction, heading downhill, soon arriving back at Round Lake. Follow the path along the lake, eventually reaching the dam. Continue hiking back to the trailhead.

Lacamas Park

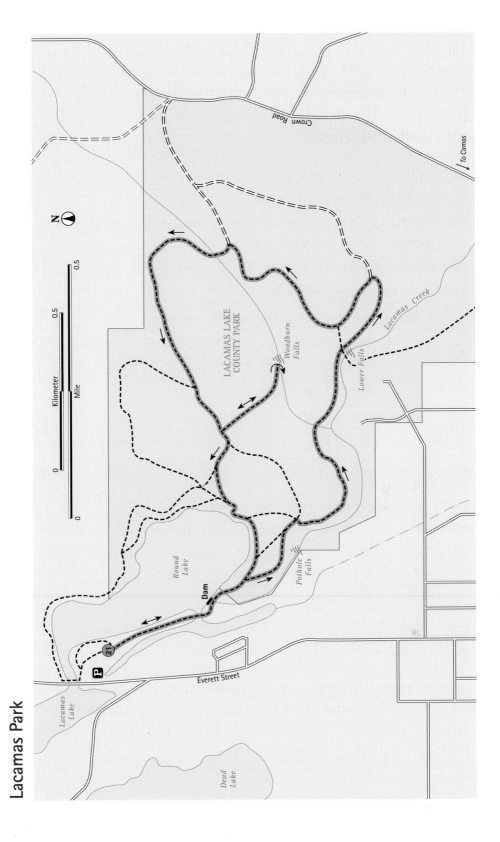

Lacamas Lake

Dead Lake

Everett Street

Lacamas Lake

Round Lake

Dam

P

21

Pothole Falls

Woodburn Falls

Lower Falls

LACAMAS LAKE COUNTY PARK

Lacamas Creek

Crown Road

To Camas

N

Kilometer

0   0.5

0   0.5   Mile

In spring and early summer, you'll want to also pay a visit to the upper meadow just off Round Lake. The Lily Trail takes you through what might just be the best wildflower viewing area in the Portland metro area.

Miles and Directions

0.0 Start at the trailhead and take the main paved path to the right, following the lake. Cross a dam and arrive at a trail junction.

0.3 Arrive at a junction on the other side of the dam. Take the path to the right, staying close to the creek.

0.4 Come to another junction. Stay right, following the creek.

0.5 Arrive at Pothole Falls; continue hiking.

0.8 Stay straight (slight right) at a junction, continuing on the main path.

1.1 Arrive at a bridge that crosses over the top of Lower Falls. Make a left, immediately passing one junction before arriving at a second.

1.2 Make a left at an access road junction.

1.6 Arrive at a T junction with a gravel road; turn left.

2.0 Reach an easy-to-miss junction on the left. Take this path to its end at Woodburn Falls, passing a junction leading left along the way. Backtrack to the gravel road and turn left.

2.6 Arrive at a junction; make a left, heading uphill.

2.7 Come to another junction and make a left, switchbacking down to Round Lake.

2.8 Arrive at a junction. Go right, staying close to the lake and arriving back at the dam. Cross the dam and hike back to the trailhead.

3.2 Arrive back at the trailhead.

Local Information

Post-hike food and drink: Top Burger Drive In, 1436 NE Everett St., or Mill City Brew Werks, 339 NE Cedar St., both in Camas, Washington

Adventure 22: Wahkeena–Multnomah Falls Loop

With combined drops cited at 630 feet, Multnomah Falls is often billed as the tallest waterfall in Oregon. Just up the road from Multnomah Falls is the much-less-heralded Wahkeena Falls. If Wahkeena were located anywhere else in Oregon, it would be a stand-alone attraction. What you miss from the road, however, is everything above both of these falls. You can visit both falls, four other named cascades, and some remarkably varied and scenic landscape by hiking the classic Wahkeena–Multnomah Falls loop.

Distance: 5.6-mile loop

Difficulty: Moderate

Trail surface: Hard-packed dirt; duffy, rocky, paved

Hiking time: 2 to 4 hours

County: Multnomah

Land status: National scenic area

Seasons: All

Trail contact: Columbia River Gorge National Scenic Area, (541) 308-1700; www.fs
.usda.gov/crgnsa

Maps: *Oregon Road & Recreation Atlas*: Page 37 F7

Finding the trailhead: From Portland, take I-84 East from Portland to exit 31 for Multnomah Falls. Find parking where you can and walk through the tunnel to the historic Multnomah Falls Lodge. Walk west about 100 feet past the lodge on the south side of the Historic Columbia River Highway to the clearly marked trailhead leading toward Wahkeena Falls. GPS: N45° 34.676' / W122° 07.189'

The Hike

Yes, there are crowds most of the year, but it never gets old seeing the expression on a visitor's face the first time he or she witnesses Multnomah Falls. Embrace it. Enjoy the giant ice-cream cookie thingy and a cup of coffee at the end of the hike. Eat a hot dog or have a sit-down dinner at the lodge and listen to others marvel over what they've just seen. Sure it's a mob scene close to the falls, but as is the case with many trails in the area, once the pavement ends the crowds thin out considerably.

The trail between Wahkeena Falls and Lemmon's Viewpoint

Starting the hike by walking away from Multnomah Falls is a bit like eating breakfast before opening presents on Christmas morning, but that's what I'm recommending here—save the best for last. Start at the Multnomah Falls Lodge and head west along the Historic Columbia River Highway. A short distance from the lodge, pick up the marked trail to Wahkeena Falls. There isn't much to this part of the trail, which is why it's good to start here; plus it's a nice warm-up.

Cross a footbridge at Wahkeena Falls and continue up along a paved path. You soon come to a stone bridge that crosses the creek within spraying distance of the falls. Continue up some long, steep switchbacks to Lemmon's Viewpoint. Enjoy the view and catch your breath before heading up the Wahkeena Canyon along the now-unpaved path. The trail marches up through the scenic canyon before arriving at small but very photogenic Fairy Falls. Hike past the falls a short distance to a junction with the Vista Point Trail. Stay right and continue on the Wahkeena Trail.

At the next junction it's worth taking a right onto the Angel's Rest Trail for about 100 yards to visit Wahkeena Springs. The spot where Wahkeena Creek

Opposite: The trail passes by Fairy Falls on the ascent through Wahkeena Canyon.

emerges from the ground also makes an excellent rest stop. There are a handful of fine lunch spots on either side of the creek here. When you're ready, go back to the Wahkeena Trail and make one last push to the top of the ridge and the end of the climbing. At the four-way junction, stay straight, passing the steep ascent to Devil's Rest on the right. If you are in the mood for a lot more exercise without a rewarding view, hoof it up to the socked-in Devil's Rest someday. Skip it this time and follow the now-level trail for 1 mile before it descends to a junction with the Larch Mountain Trail. Turn left here, following Multnomah Creek as it passes Ecola, Weisendanger, and Dutchman Falls on its way to a small bridge crossing. This is arguably the most scenic and dynamic segment of the hike. Just after the crossing, the pavement begins again and meets a two-way junction. Take the short jaunt to the left to visit the viewing platform at the top of Multnomah Falls. Return to the main path and ascend briefly before beginning the paved 1-mile-long descent to the base of Multnomah Falls and the end of the hike.

Miles and Directions

0.0 Start from Multnomah Falls Lodge; head west along the Historic Columbia River Highway and pick up the marked trail to Wahkeena Falls.

0.3 Arrive at the Wahkeena Falls Trailhead; continue up the paved path.

0.6 Arrive at Wahkeena Falls Bridge; continue up the paved path.

2.3 Continue up switchbacks to Lemmon's Viewpoint (N45° 34.445' / W122° 07.600'). The paved trail ends. Hike up along Wahkeena Creek, passing Fairy Falls (N45° 34.215' / W122° 07.481') and a junction with the Vista Point Trail, arriving at a junction with the Angel's Rest Trail. Take a right and arrive a short time later at Wahkeena Springs. Head back to the junction.

3.4 Continue east on the Wahkeena Trail and past a junction leading to Devil's Rest, arriving at a junction with the Larch Mountain Trail.

4.1 Make a left at the junction and head downstream following Multnomah Creek. Pass Ecola (N45° 34.455' / W122° 06.437'), Weisendanger (N45° 34.491' / W122° 06.474'), and Dutchman Falls (N45° 34.552' / W122° 06.597') before crossing a small footbridge and arriving at a junction leading to the Multnomah Falls viewing platform. If you would like to see the falls from above, walk down to the platform. Otherwise, stay right.

Wahkeena–Multnomah Falls Loop

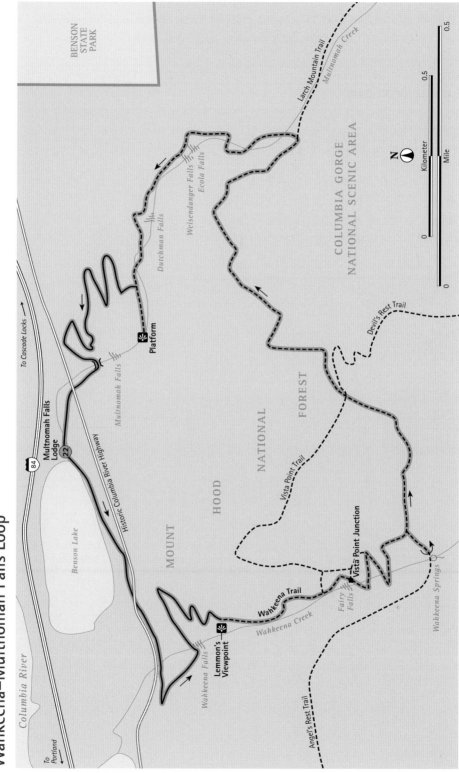

5.6 Descend several paved switchbacks, cross the Benson Bridge at Multnomah Falls (N45° 34.603' / W122° 06.984'), and arrive back at the lodge.

Local Information

Post-hike food and drink: Multnomah Falls Lodge is pretty good, if a bit overpriced. You could always hit up McMenamins Edgefield, 2126 SW Halsey St., Troutdale, on the way back into town.

Adventure 23: Oneonta Gorge

This little adventure is indeed one of a kind. The Oneonta Gorge is a slot canyon barely 0.6 mile long in the Columbia River Gorge. Designated a botanical area by the USDA Forest Service, the steep basalt walls of the canyon are home to numerous rare plants and an incredibly scenic waterfall. At just over a mile round-trip, this hike doesn't set any distance records, but burning lungs and thigh muscles aren't why people visit this falls.

Distance: 1.2 miles out and back
Difficulty: Moderate
Trail surface: Creek bed; water; rocky
Hiking time: 1 to 2 hours
County: Multnomah
Land status: National scenic area
Seasons: Summer
Trail contact: Columbia River Gorge National Scenic Area, (541) 308-1700; www.fs
.usda.gov/crgnsa

Looking down the Oneonta Gorge from the logjam

Maps: *Oregon Road & Recreation Atlas:* Page 37 F7

Finding the trailhead: From Portland, take I–84 East to exit 35. Follow the Historic Columbia River Highway 2 miles to a parking area just past the recently reopened Oneonta Tunnel. Walk down a set of stairs located just before the bridge and begin making your way upstream. GPS: N45° 35.372' / W122° 04.534'

The Hike

The moment you descend the staircase leading to Oneonta Creek, you're welcomed with an air temperature that can be as much as 20 degrees cooler than where you parked. There may be no better place in the Columbia River Gorge on a hot summer day! The cool canyon is narrow, with 100-foot walls of rock on either side. First things first, however; you have to get up, over, or around a large logjam that changes with each season. Exercise caution here and gauge your hiking party's abilities. Though children frequently make this journey under the watchful eye of parents, this is very much a personal judgment call. Once the jam has been negotiated, the actual journey begins. Don't bother looking for a trail here—Oneonta Creek is the trail. This is definitely a warm-weather

Lower Oneonta Falls

Oneonta Gorge

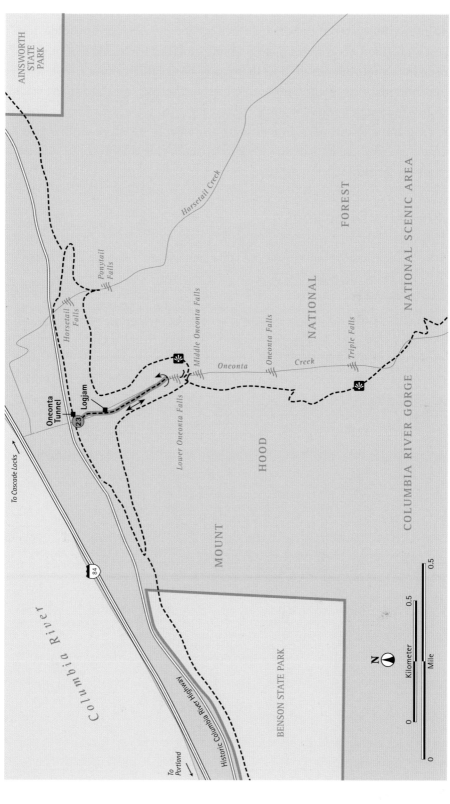

Columbia River

To Cascade Locks

To Portland

Historic Columbia River Highway

Oneonta Tunnel

Logjam

23

Horsetail Falls

Ponytail Falls

Horsetail Creek

AINSWORTH STATE PARK

Middle Oneonta Falls

Lower Oneonta Falls

Oneonta Falls

Oneonta Creek

Triple Falls

MOUNT HOOD

NATIONAL

FOREST

BENSON STATE PARK

COLUMBIA RIVER GORGE

NATIONAL SCENIC AREA

N

Kilometer 0 0.5

Mile 0 0.5

adventure. The water in the shaded creek is cold and ranges from ankle deep to chest high. Good water shoes, a bathing suit, and the love of cold mountain water are definitely recommended. Now that you've been sufficiently scared, know that most folks make it out and back without issue. Shortly after the deepest wading, the 100-foot-high Lower Oneonta Falls emerges from around a corner. The falls are long and elegant, with an invitingly swimmable splash pool. This area can become crowded on hot summer weekends, but having this grotto to yourself on a weekday is magical.

Miles and Directions

0.0   Start by walking down the staircase at the west end of the Oneonta Creek Bridge. Proceed upstream and over the logjam. Continue creek walking and wading upstream.

0.6   Arrive at the base of Lower Oneonta Falls (N45° 35.181' / W122° 04.379'). Head back the way you came.

1.2   Arrive back at the trailhead.

Adventure 24: Wahclella Falls

Wahclella Falls receives far fewer visitors than the average Columbia River Gorge waterfall, perhaps due to the falls' lack of stature and visibility, as well as length of the hike. The second and most visible 60-foot drop of the falls occupies a peaceful grotto at the end of a deep canyon. Although hikers feeling the need for more exercise often overlook it, Wahclella rates as high as any hike in the area in terms of beauty if not distance.

Distance: 2.0-mile lollipop

Difficulty: Easy

Trail surface: Gravel, hard-packed dirt; rocky

Hiking time: 1 to 2 hours

County: Multnomah

Land status: State park

Seasons: All

Fees and permits: Northwest Forest Pass or day-use fee

A thundering Wahclella Falls

Trail contact: Oregon Parks and Recreation Department, (800) 551-6949; oregon
  stateparks.org

Maps: *Oregon Road & Recreation Atlas:* Page 37 E8

Finding the trailhead: From Portland, take I-84 East to exit 40 for the Bonneville
  Dam. Turn right and go 100 yards to the turnaround and parking area. GPS: N45°
  37.817' / W121° 57.235'

The Hike

This easy lollipop hike allows hikers of almost any age and aptitude the opportunity to explore and enjoy the canyon's many attributes. The trail starts alongside
Tanner Creek on a roadbed until the road ends near a small dam that diverts water
to a fish hatchery downstream. From here the trail begins to head upstream, but
not before a bridge takes you within arm's reach of another 68-foot waterfall,
Munra Falls. Munra looks as much like a water-park slide as it does a naturally
occurring cascade, and it will often give you a light misting in late winter and
spring.

The hike along Tanner Creek

Wahclella Falls

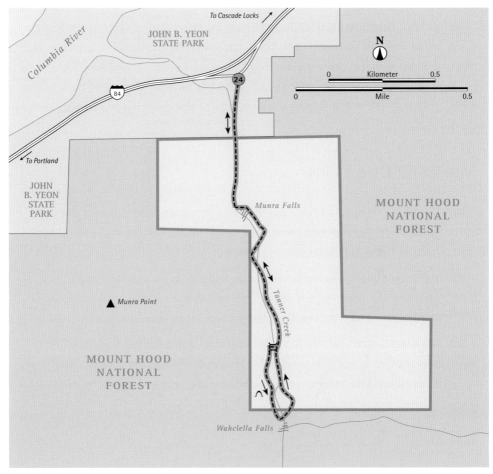

The trail forks around the 0.8-mile mark. Either direction leads to the falls, but take the trail to the right that descends back down to the creek and a long wooden bridge. This is a great spot to observe the gigantic boulders that re-formed the creek after a landslide in 1973. The building-size obstructions created a series of mini-falls and pools. Continuing upstream, the sound of Wahclella can soon be heard echoing through the canyon; you'll catch your first glimpse of the falls soon after. Now the area opens up and becomes endlessly explorable. There are boulders to climb and small pools to wade through. Be mindful, however, that this is still a dangerously fast-moving creek in spots. There is even a mini-cave just before a bridge that recrosses the creek on its way to the falls. You can't go back too far, but younger hikers often refuse to pass by without inspecting the darkness.

After the bridge the trail leads up to a rocky viewpoint of the falls. While the main tier of the falls is only 60 feet high, the water is forced out of a narrow slot that produces an impressive thundering water-hose effect. From here there are a number of convoluted trail options to follow, but all bootpaths lead back to the main trail. Follow the trail along the east side of the creek back downstream to the trailhead.

Miles and Directions

0.0   Start at the trailhead and head upstream on a wide gravel road. Continue past a water intake dam and cross a footbridge next to Munra Falls (N45° 37.575' / W121° 57.208'). Proceed along the trail to a junction.

0.8   Either route will lead to the falls before looping back to the junction. For the described hike, bear right and descend to a long footbridge crossing Tanner Creek. Continue along the trail, crossing another bridge before arriving at Wahclella Falls.

1.0   Arrive at Wahclella Falls (N45° 37.104' / W121° 57.084'). The trail leads up to the falls and then ascends the canyon wall, heading downstream on the east side of Tanner Creek. Stay straight at the trail junction and continue back to the trailhead.

2.0   Arrive back at the trailhead.

Adventure 25: Eagle Creek

Built in 1915, the Eagle Creek Trail opened in conjunction with the Historic Columbia River Highway. The trail leads through one of the most sensational canyons in the entire Columbia River Gorge. Along the way you'll travel a path that was blasted out of basalt cliffs, visit numerous waterfalls, and cross bridges that offer spectacular views of chasms below. The trail is well kept, often wide, and gently graded, making it a great option for novices. There are, however, a couple of sections where the trail is narrow and exposed. Cabling is provided in these sections to help ease your mind, but you still might want to proceed with caution. As an added bonus, October and November are prime times to watch salmon making their way upstream to spawn. Eagle Creek is one of the premier spots in the Columbia River Gorge to witness this marvel of nature. Some of the best viewing is available at the trailhead and along the creek's first stretch of hiking.

Distance: 4.2 miles out and back to Punchbowl Falls; 12.5 miles out and back to Tunnel Falls; 13.5 miles out and back to 7 Mile Falls

Difficulty: Easy to difficult

Trail surface: Hard-packed dirt; duffy, rocky

Hiking time: 2 to 8 hours

County: Hood River

Land status: State park

Seasons: All. Though some portions of the trail have a propensity to get icy in winter, particularly the sections with the most exposure. Exercise caution and come prepared.

Fees and permits: Northwest Forest Pass or day-use fee

Trail contact: Oregon Parks and Recreation Department, (800) 551-6949; oregon stateparks.org

Maps: *Oregon Road & Recreation Atlas:* Page 37, E8

Finding the trailhead: From Portland, take I-84 East to exit 41 and turn right at the bottom of the exit. Travel 0.6 mile along a narrow road to the parking area and trailhead (GPS: N45° 38.208' / W121° 55.175'). If that parking area is full, park back at the parking area near the front of the park.

The Hike

As with many out-and-back hikes, you have options with regard to how long you want your outing to be. And based on how tired or spry you're feeling, you can always call an audible. The three recommended options are a 4.2-mile stroll up to Punchbowl Falls, a 12.5-mile hike to Tunnel Falls, or a 13.5-mile trek to 7 Mile Falls. You can take 0.5 mile off the last two options if you cut out the side trips to Metlako and Punchbowl.

From the trailhead hike 1.5 miles to a junction with a side trail on the right leading down to a viewpoint of Metlako Falls. After the falls continue another 0.3 mile along the main path to the junction with the Lower Punchbowl Trail. Take this trail down 0.25 mile to Punchbowl Falls and Lower Punchbowl Falls. This is the turnaround point for the 4.2-mile hike option.

To get to Tunnel Falls, return to the main path and continue to High Bridge. From there hike another 2.7 miles, passing several nice lunch spots and small, scenic cascades before arriving at Tunnel Falls. This one-of-a-kind 120-foot cascade features a tunnel chipped through solid rock that goes literally behind the falls. If you've made it this far, I highly recommend that you continue to the

Punchbowl Falls

The view from the trail, high above Eagle Creek

two waterfalls after Tunnel. In addition to bonus waterfalls, this final 0.6-mile stretch is some of the most scenic of the hike. Just 0.3 mile past Tunnel Falls waits the aptly named Twister Falls. Just above Twister Falls is a great area for lunch or a snack break. Another 0.2 mile later you'll arrive at 7 Mile Falls and the official turnaround point. Head back the way you came.

Miles and Directions

0.0   Start at the trailhead and follow the trail up the east side of Eagle Creek. Look for a spur trail (N45° 37.627' / W121° 53.816') to the Metlako Falls viewpoint (N45° 37.637' / W121° 53.856') at the 1.6-mile mark.

1.8   Arrive at a junction with the Lower Punchbowl Trail. Make a right here and hike steeply down to the water and Lower Punchbowl Falls (N45° 37.382' / W121° 53.716') and a view of Punchbowl Falls (N45° 37.340' / W121° 53.677'). Back at the main trail, continue to the right, passing an upper viewpoint for Punchbowl Falls as well as Loowit Falls (N45° 36.522' / W121° 53.073') just before arriving at High Bridge.

Eagle Creek

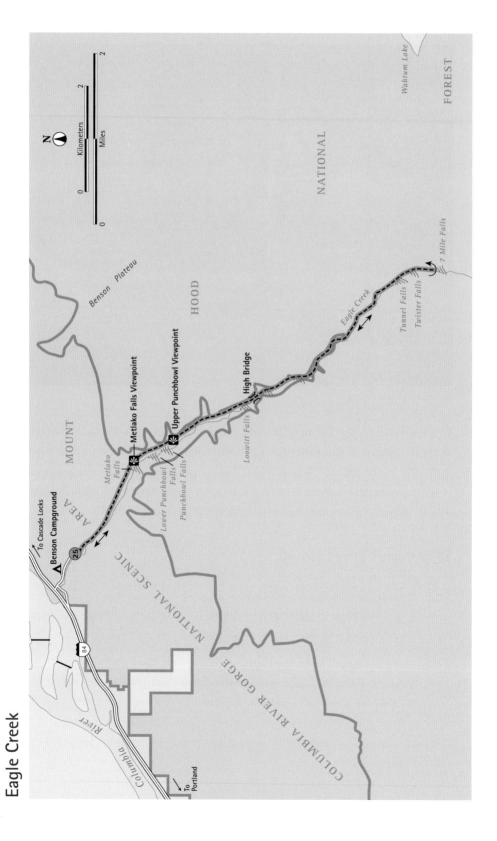

3.7 Arrive at High Bridge; continue along the trail.

6.5 Reach Tunnel Falls (N45° 35.118' / W121° 51.140'). Continue another 0.3 mile to Twister Falls (N45° 34.922' / W121° 51.161').

6.8 Reach Twister Falls. Continue 0.2 mile to 7 Mile Falls (N45° 34.692' / W121° 51.128').

7.0 Arrive at 7 Mile Falls. Head back the way you came.

13.5 Arrive back at the trailhead.

Adventure 26: Falls Creek Falls

Truly one of the megastars of southwest Washington, the list of superlatives that have been used to describe Falls Creek Falls is indeed a long one. It doesn't matter that it's not possible to see all 335 feet of the three-tiered monster at the same time. The size, power, and visual appeal of Falls Creek Falls are something to behold, whether you're gazing at the top tier or the bottom two. Combine the fact that there are a number of good spots from which to sit and take in the falls with the easy-to-digest length of 3.2 total miles, and you have a classic day hike perfect for the family or to show off to out-of-towners.

Distance: 3.2 miles out and back with a 6.3-mile loop option

Difficulty: Easy to moderate

Trail surface: Hard-packed dirt; duffy, rocky

Hiking time: 1.5 to 3 hours

County: Skamania

Land status: National forest

Seasons: Spring, summer, and fall; gate is locked Dec–Mar.

Fees and permits: Toll bridge

Trail contact: Gifford Pinchot National Forest, Mount Adams Ranger District, Trout Lake, Washington; (509) 395-3400; www.fs.usda.gov/recarea/giffordpinchot/recarea/?recid=31184

Maps: *DeLorme: Washington Atlas & Gazetteer:* Page 100 A5

Finding the trailhead: From Portland, take I-84 East to exit 44 for Cascade Locks. Cross the Bridge of the Gods (toll) and turn right onto WA 14. After 6 miles turn left to go through Carson. After another 14.5 miles, turn right, following a sign for Mount St. Helens. Almost 1 mile later, bear right onto gravel FR 3062 and drive 2 miles to its dead end at the Lower Falls parking area (GPS: N43° 18.800' / W122° 50.117'). There is a seasonal gate closure here December through March.

The Hike

From the trailhead the path begins wide and easy through second-growth forest. Stay straight, ignoring a trail to the left after 200 feet. The trail soon arrives at Falls Creek, and with the exception of just a couple of cutaways, the path parallels

Opposite: The middle and lower tier of Falls Creek Falls

PANTHER CREEK FALLS

Panther Creek Falls is arguably one of the most jaw-dropping waterfalls any-where in the Northwest. Imagine a giant natural spring composed of 100 feet or so of intertwining ribbons of water and moss, gently flowing down the face of a massive basalt wall. Now also picture a pristine creek rushing toward that palisade, with a small segment of the stream splintering off just prior to impact, creating a delicate, veil-like cascade. Meanwhile the majority of the creek careens into the spring, becoming a turbulent 70-foot waterfall. Once united, the waters travel a very short distance before falling over a lower 30-foot tier. This is Panther Creek Falls.

From Carson, take Wind River Road north for 5.8 miles to Old State Road. Turn right and then make an immediate left onto Panther Creek Road. Drive along Panther Creek Road for 7.4 miles to a large gravel pit on the right side of the road; park here. There is no marked trailhead, and there may or may not be signage indicating the waterfall. Cross the road and start walking south, or the direction you came from, for about 150 feet to the easy-to-miss trail on the side of the road.

The path descends quickly and leads to a large viewing platform roughly 150 yards from the trailhead. A scramble path about 75 feet to the left (south) side of the viewing platform leads down to the base of the falls. It is, however, a very steep and dangerous path, made all the more so in wet conditions. It

the creek or stays within earshot for the duration of the hike. After 0.4 mile of hiking, cross over a footbridge that offers a great view of Falls Creek as it squeezes through a narrow gorge. The trail now enters old-growth forest and begins gently rolling, ascending, and descending along the scenic creek. The path occasionally dips in and out of ravines and stays well graded for another 0.5 mile or so. Sharp eyes will spot tiny calypso orchids along the trail here in late spring and early summer. Also known as fairy slippers, these tiny purple orchids only thrive in undisturbed forest.

The path then begins gaining elevation more greedily, pausing briefly at a junction with the upper trail. Save this potential add-on for the way back. The upper trail gives you a heaping helping of extra elevation, but a somewhat tanta-lizingly disappointing view of Falls Creek Falls' upper tier. For now, stay straight and continue toward the falls. In 0.2 mile more you'll encounter a bridge crossing

A steep scramble path leads to the base of Panther Creek Falls.

requires a couple of rock-climbing maneuvers and a certain level of off-trail experience.

over a creek that ranges from thundering in spring to bone-dry in late summer. After the bridge gain one last little chunk of elevation and cross another creek, bridgeless this time. This mini-creek has the potential to moisten your feet in spring, though it's usually a relatively easy rock-hop. This one also dries out pretty well with warmer weather. After the mini-creek crossing, the trail rounds a bend and the falls become audible. Look carefully through the trees over the next 100 yards or so—there are a couple good views of Falls Creek Falls' elusive upper tier and the top of the second tier. The upper tier will not be visible from where the trail ends near the base of the falls.

The trail now loses elevation over the last 500 feet before arriving at Falls Creek Falls. The view here is of the middle and lower tiers of the cascade, but you won't feel like you're missing anything. They are both graceful and thunderous. Explore the space, have a picnic, and head back the way you came. If you are

Falls Creek from the trail

content with the falls, continue all the way back to the trailhead. If you'd like a little more forest time and a lot more exercise, hang a right at the junction with the Upper Falls Trail, marked #152. Climb a steep 0.2 mile to a T junction and turn right onto the Upper Falls Trail. Hike 0.9 mile more to the Upper Falls viewpoint. As mentioned, it doesn't offer much of a view of the falls, though there are some sketchy scramble paths in the area if you want to attempt to gain a clearer look.

To complete the loop, hike back the way you came and stay straight, remaining on the upper trail when you encounter the junction leading back down to the lower trail. Hike a total of 2.6 miles from the Upper Falls viewpoint to a junction and turn left, crossing the creek on a footbridge. Turn left after the bridge and head upstream along a scenic stretch of Falls Creek for another 0.6 mile to a final junction. Turn right here and arrive at the trailhead a quick 300 feet or so later.

Falls Creek Falls

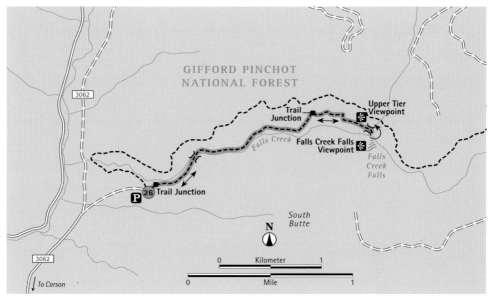

Miles and Directions

0.0 Start at the trailhead and hike to a bridge crossing.

0.4 Cross Falls Creek on a wooden footbridge and continue hiking.

1.2 At a junction (N43° 18.945' / W122° 50.162') with the Upper Falls Trail, stay straight.

1.6 Arrive at Falls Creek Falls. Head back the way you came.

3.2 Arrive back at the trailhead.

Loop Option:

The longer loop directions continue below, beginning at Falls Creek Falls (milepoint 1.6).

2.0 At a junction with the Upper Falls Trail, marked #152, turn right and climb steeply.

2.2 At another junction, turn right.

3.1 Arrive at the Upper Falls viewpoint. Head back the way you came.

4.0 At the junction leading back down to the Lower Falls, stay straight.

5.7 Turn left at the junction and cross Falls Creek on a footbridge. Turn left after the bridge and continue hiking.

6.3 At the next junction, turn right and continue for about 300 feet to the trailhead.

Local Information

Post-hike food and drink: Backwoods Brewing Company, 1162B Wind River Highway, Carson, Washington

Adventure 27: Dog Mountain

Dog Mountain is one of the most popular spring hiking destinations in the entire region. Generations have made this hike a Memorial Day weekend staple. For others, it's a celebration of spring featuring one of the best wildflower displays in the Columbia River Gorge. The upper meadows of Dog Mountain explode with color in May and June. The trail is also an early-season conditioning hike for those looking to summit Cascade peaks later in the year. This 7-mile, 2,900-foot elevation gain loop hike makes an excellent primer. Team all of that up with picturesque classic Gorge views, and you've got a recipe for a crowded parking lot. If you're hiking Dog Mountain on a sunny May or June weekend, prepare to get acquainted with several of your outdoor loving neighbors. If you prefer to have the trail to yourself, leave early on a weekday.

> Distance: 7.0-mile loop
> Difficulty: Moderate to difficult
> Trail surface: Hard-packed dirt; duffy, rocky
> Hiking time: 2.5 to 5 hours
> County: Skamania
> Land status: National forest
> Seasons: All, best in May and June
> Fees and permits: Toll bridge
> Trail contact: US Forest Service, Columbia River Gorge National Scenic Area. http://fs.usda.gov/crgnsa
> Maps: *DeLorme: Washington Atlas & Gazetteer:* Page 101 C6
> Finding the trailhead: From Portland, take I-84 East to exit 44 for Cascade Locks. Cross the Bridge of the Gods (toll) and make a right onto WA 14. Drive 12 miles to mile marker 53.5 and look for the signed pull-off on the left.

The Hike

The hike begins at the far right end of the parking lot. Head up past the restrooms and begin climbing, and climbing, and climbing some more. After 0.5 mile stay right at a junction, avoiding the "Old Trail." Continue another 1 mile to the lower meadows viewpoint. In spring the meadows are dominated by yellow balsamroot, with patches of purple lupine. But those are just the headliners; keep your eyes open, because there's a lot of variety up here. If you've had enough, this is a

The trail approaches the upper meadows of Dog Mountain.

great spot to have a snack and turn back. What you've just accomplished makes for a sturdy 3-mile, 1,500-foot elevation gain option.

If the summit is your destination, hike uphill another 0.5 mile until you rejoin the Old Trail. Put in 0.5 mile of steep climbing to reach the site of an old lookout tower and the beginning of the final ascent. The trail splits here; either way will reach the top. The trail to the left is far more scenic, however. One more 0.5-mile stretch and you've reached the summit. You'll want a break at this point, and this summit is a particularly good place to do it. Across the river, Mount Defiance, the tallest mountain in the Gorge, lords over the Columbia River. Just west of you, Wind Mountain looks a little more attainable. To continue the loop, head down the Augspurger Trail. After about 1 mile you'll encounter another junction. Turn left and enjoy the gentle grade of the final 2.8 miles to the parking lot.

Miles and Directions

0.0   Start from the east end of the parking area and begin hiking up the trail to walk the loop in a counterclockwise direction.

Dog Mountain

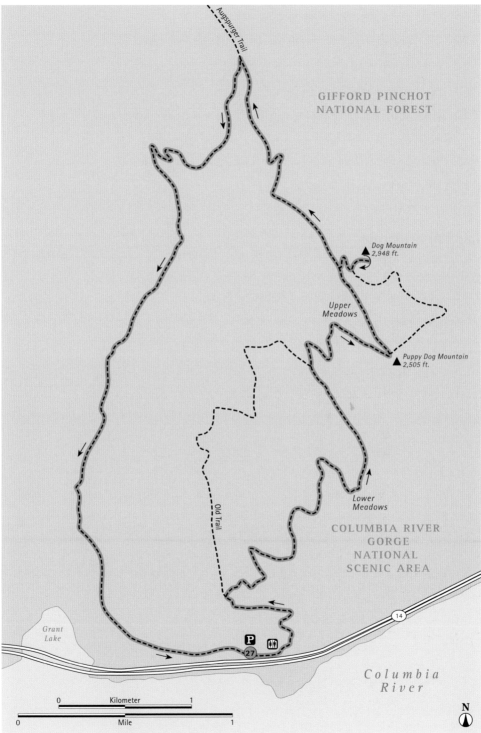

GIFFORD PINCHOT
NATIONAL FOREST

Augspurger Trail

Dog Mountain
2,948 ft.

Upper
Meadows

Puppy Dog Mountain
2,505 ft.

Old Trail

Lower
Meadows

COLUMBIA RIVER
GORGE
NATIONAL
SCENIC AREA

14

Grant
Lake

P

27

Columbia
River

0   Kilometer   1

0   Mile   1

N

0.6 Arrive at a junction with the Old Trail. Stay to the right.

1.6 Arrive at the lower meadows. Continue up.

2.2 Come to a second junction with the Old Trail. Stay to the right.

2.7 At a junction make a hard left, hiking through the upper meadows.

3.1 Reach a junction and make a right.

3.2 Arrive at the Dog Mountain summit. Hike back down to the last junction and make a right.

4.2 Reach a junction leading to Augspurger Mountain. Make a left.

7.0 Arrive back at the trailhead.

Local Information

Post-hike food and drink: In Stevenson, Washington, check out Andrew's Pizza, 310 SW 2nd St., or Walking Man Brewing Co., 240 SW 1st St.

Adventure 28: Trail of Ten Falls (Silver Falls State Park)

Silver Falls State Park offers a diverse array of services, from primitive campgrounds and cabins to horse corrals and a conference center. But really, it's all about the waterfalls. The crown jewel of the park is the Trail of Ten Falls, a loop hike arguably as spectacular and scenic as any in Oregon. During this epic outing you'll pass by no fewer than ten waterfalls ranging in height from 27 to 177 feet. And, yes, the waterfalls are the primary draw, but beautiful forest, deep opal pools of water, and striking canyon views rank highly as well. Another asset is the flexibility to choose where to start and how far to hike.

Distance: 8.2-mile loop (5.2-mile option)

Difficulty: Moderate to difficult

Trail surface: Paved, hard-packed dirt; rocky

Hiking time: 1.5 to 5 hours

County: Marion

Land status: State park

Seasons: All

Fees and permits: Day-use fee

Trail contact: Oregon Parks and Recreation Department, (503) 986-0707; oregon
  stateparks.org

Maps: *Oregon Road & Recreation Atlas:* Page 48 F5

Finding the trailhead: From downtown Salem, head east on State Street and drive
  11.8 miles. Turn right onto Cascade Highway SE and drive 3.6 miles. Turn left
  onto the Silver Falls Highway and drive 7.8 miles, arriving at Silver Falls State
  Park. The described hike starts from the South Falls parking area. GPS: N44°
  52.748' / W122° 39.401'

The Hike

There are two main trailheads and a third with a 2-hour parking limit to choose from, giving you the option of reducing the hike to a more manageable 5.2-mile loop that still passes most of the larger falls. I recommend starting at the South Falls parking area and taking the Rim Trail toward Winter Falls. This might seem counterintuitive, since it leads you away from South Falls, the largest waterfall

Lower South Falls

on the trail. It's all a matter of personal preference, but I enjoy the "best for last" approach.

If you're taking the shorter loop, turn left onto the Winter Falls Trail when you arrive at the Winter Falls Trailhead; then turn left again when you reach a junction with the Canyon Trail. The path will loop back to South Falls and the South Falls parking area.

If you're making the full loop and it's high-water season, it's worth taking the steep path down to the base of Winter Falls for the full view. If it's late summer and you don't feel like hoofing it down to the base and back up, nobody will hold it against you. Continue past Winter Falls on the Rim Trail, making your way up to North Falls. When you reach the junction at North Falls, take the short 0.2-mile jaunt to the right to visit Upper North Falls and then return to the massive North Falls. The trail descends to and behind the thundering North Falls. Continuing along the Canyon Trail, the scenery in the deep canyon is stunning, and you're seemingly greeted by a new cascade around every turn.

The trail eventually loops back to epic South Falls. The path becomes paved and climbs up to and behind the imposing cascade. Keep an eye out for tree wells when you're behind the falls. These round holes in the ceilings of the caverns

Trail of Ten Falls (Silver Falls State Park)

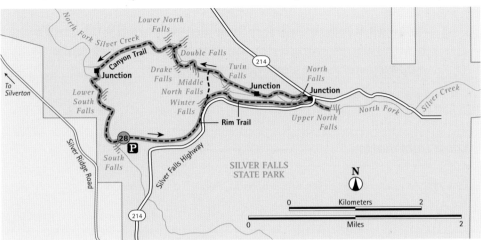

behind the falls were formed millions of years ago. Occasionally a lava flow would encounter a tree and harden around it while the tree eventually burned away. Water erosion did the rest, moving soil from underneath the lava rock and leaving behind tree wells. Keep looking up and you'll spot a few. Continue up the paved path and back to the parking area where you started.

Miles and Directions

0.0   Start from the South Falls parking area. Hike up the Rim Trail toward Winter Falls, away from South Falls.

1.2   Arrive at the Winter Falls Trailhead (N44° 53.065' / W122° 38.434'). Head down to the left to view the falls. Continue easterly along the Rim Trail. (*Option:* For a shorter loop, make a left at the junction with the Canyon Trail and continue on this path until you arrive back at the parking area at 5.2 miles.)

2.3   Reach the junction with North Falls. Take the short trip to the right to visit Upper North Falls (N44° 52.979' / W122° 36.935') and then return to North Falls (N44° 53.119' / W122° 37.374'). Take the descending Canyon Trail and continue to Twin Falls (N44° 53.133' / W122° 38.226'). Continue hiking to a junction.

4.6   Arrive at the junction with the Winter Falls Trail. Continue straight. Stay on the Canyon Trail at any junctions, visiting Middle North Falls (N44° 53.343' / W122° 38.596'), Drake Falls (N44° 53.350' / W122° 38.786'), Double Falls (N44° 53.517' /

W122° 38.732'), Lower North Falls (N44° 53.466' / W122° 38.843'), and Lower South Falls (N44° 53.115' / W122° 39.702') along the way.

7.7 Stay straight at a junction just before South Falls (N44° 52.781' / W122° 39.498'). The paved path then leads behind the falls and ascends back up to the parking area where you started the hike.

8.2 Arrive back at the parking area.

Local Information

Post-hike food and drink: Seven Brides Brewing, 990 N 1st St., Silverton

PADDLING

O ne of the things the Northwest is known for is water. The western side of the Cascades undoubtedly gets its fair share of precipitation. Sure, it makes for some gray days, but all that water does more than make the grass green. With an almost countless number of lakes, swimming holes, sloughs, creeks, and rivers, the greater Portland area is heaven for those who like to have a paddle or an oar in their hands. And that should include you. If you are an outdoor enthusiast and you're not taking advantage of the water here, you're doing it wrong. But I digress. Ask one hundred different people for a rundown of the best paddles in the area and you'll get one hundred different lists. And while these are my favorites, they're just the tip of the iceberg.

Ross Island, with downtown Portland in the distance

Recommended Outfitters and Guide Services

Next Adventure. If you're hiking, climbing, paddling, skiing, disc golfing, or pretty much anything besides underwater basket weaving, Next Adventure can square you up. They also offer a number of paddle sport programs for every type of paddling we have in the area (nextadventure.net/portland-kayak-school .html).

Alder Creek Kayak & Canoe. Specializing in paddle sports, Alder Creek is the place to buy or rent gear, get expert advice, or learn how and where to paddle (aldercreek.com).

Adventure 29: Smith and Bybee Lakes

The Smith and Bybee Lakes area is the nation's largest urban freshwater wetland. Tucked into North Portland's industrial area, this is perhaps the best place to spot birds within the city. The lakes combine to make around 200 acres of explorable but shallow paddling. As a result, these lakes are generally better to explore in winter through early summer.

County: Multnomah

Put-in: Near the end of the road, past the restrooms

Takeout: Same as put-in

Distance: Self-dependent

Float time: Self-dependent

Difficulty rating: Easy

Rapids: None

Waterway type: Lakes

Current: None

River gradient: N/A

River gauge: N/A

Land status: City park

Nearest town: Portland

Boats used: Canoe or kayak

Seasons: Best in spring and winter

Fees and permits: None

Schedule: 24/7

Maps: *Oregon Road & Recreation Atlas:* Page 106 B3

Getting there: From downtown Portland, take I-5 North to exit 307 for Marine Drive. Turn right onto Marine Drive and continue just under 1 mile to the Smith and Bybee Wetlands Natural Area parking lot, on the left. Drive past the restrooms to a small pullout near a barricade at the end of the road. Follow the marked path down to the lake. GPS: N45° 36.759' / W122° 42.794'

The Paddle

Hidden in the middle of the warehouses and port terminals of the North Portland peninsula, the Smith and Bybee Wetlands are home to several wildlife species, including some you might not expect. Bald eagles, beavers, and one of the

A fall morning on Smith Lake

last remaining large populations of western painted turtles in Oregon all reside in the wetlands. A long list of the usual suspects also call the natural area home, including black-tailed deer and an ever-changing lineup of seasonal birds.

With more than 200 acres of interconnected lakes and channels that don't allow motorboats and the semi-secluded location, you're pretty much guaranteed a peaceful paddle. From the put-in, the area is your oyster. But navigation can be a bit tricky, so take note of your surroundings once on the water if you'd like to find your way out.

Water levels vary greatly by season, from flood-level stage in late winter to muddy bog in late summer. In fact, paddling might not even be possible by the end of summer. Your best bet is to head out anytime in spring or winter, which both happen to offer excellent wildlife viewing as well. The paddling here is easy and self-guided. Depending on water levels, it is possible to make your way from Smith Lake into Bybee Lake.

For many, peace and birds are the main attractions here. You may see the occasional plane from PDX or a truck heading down Marine Drive, but in terms

Opposite: The trail leading to the put-in on Smith Lake

Smith and Bybee Lakes

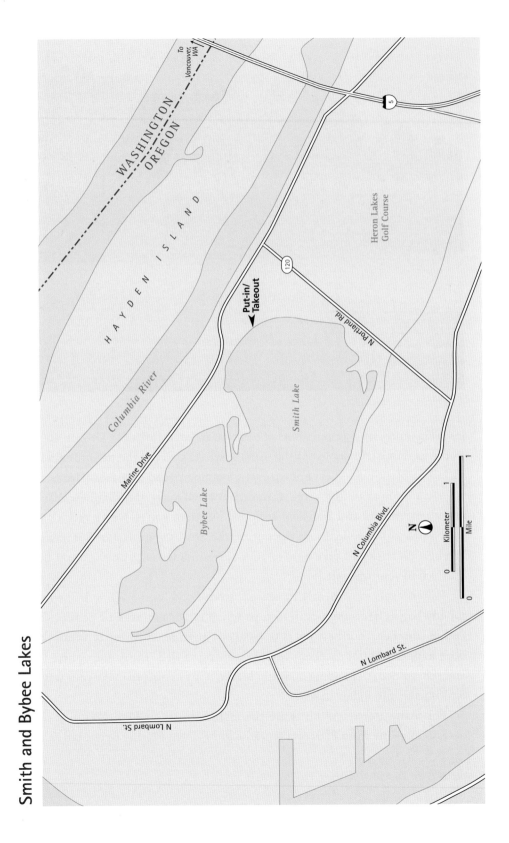

of an urban paddle, this is about as peaceful as you're going to get. It sometimes seems as though nobody knows the natural area is here. It's vast, and motorized engines are not allowed on the lakes, making them all the more inviting for paddlers.

The Smith and Bybee Lakes are a prime spot if don't have a lot of time but still want a quality paddle in nature. If you're on a time crunch, North Portland isn't *that* far away, no matter what your friends living in Inner Southeast say. And if you're into wildlife, particularly birds, this spot is one of Portland's birding meccas.

Local Information

Post-paddle food and drink: In St. Johns, check out Slim's Cocktail Bar & Restaurant, 8635 N Lombard St., or Thai Cottage, 8620 N Lombard St.

Adventure 30: Ross Island

Flatwater trips don't get any closer to downtown Portland than the river that cuts through the heart of it. The paddle around Ross Island is an urban favorite for a fistful of reasons, not the least of which are convenience, stunning city views, and a surprisingly vast array of wildlife.

County: Multnomah

Put-in: At either Sellwood Riverfront Park or Willamette Park

Takeout: Same as put-in

Distance: Self-dependent

Float time: 0.5 to 2 hours

Difficulty rating: Easy

Rapids: None

Waterway type: Wide, deep river; lots of boat traffic

Current: Minimal

River gradient: N/A

River gauge: N/A

Land status: City park (Ross Island)

Nearest town: Portland

Boats used: Canoe or kayak

Season: Spring through fall

Fees and permits: None

Schedule: N/A

Maps: *Oregon Road & Recreation Atlas:* Page 106 E4–5

Getting there: If you're starting on the east side of the river, it's probably easier to put in at Sellwood Riverfront Park. Take Mcloughlin Boulevard to SE Tacoma Street and follow SE Tacoma west to SE 7th Avenue. Turn right onto SE 7th, followed by an immediate left onto SE Spokane Street. Make a right onto SE Oaks Park Way and turn left into Sellwood Riverfront Park. Park and follow the path down to the water and the put-in at the dock. GPS: N45° 27.966' / W122° 39.849'

If you're starting on the west side of the river, put in at Willamette Park. Head south on SW Macadam Avenue to SW Nebraska Street. Make a left here and then a quick right onto SW Beaver Avenue. The parking and put-in areas are on the left. GPS: N45° 28.532' / W122° 40.133'

THE PADDLE

The Ross Island paddle is an urban favorite among canoers and kayakers. A contingent of stand-up paddlers favor the trek as well. Sitting smack dab in the middle of the Willamette River where the waterway bends around downtown, Ross Island, like many of Portland's natural areas, is teeming with wildlife. Over one hundred species of birds inhabit the island during migration, including bald eagle, osprey, and blue heron, as well as black-tailed deer, river otter, and beaver.

From either put-in, paddle downriver, which in this case happens to be north, toward the island. The island itself sports a rather large lagoon. The 100-foot-deep lagoon is the result of mining that ceased in the 1990s. Though the mining has stopped, sand and gravel are still being processed on parts of the island. How you make your way to the island is entirely up to you, but the Holgate Channel on the east side of Ross Island is your best bet. The south end of the channel is a no-wake zone and is much more scenic as it squeezes between the island and the Oaks Bottom Wildlife Refuge. However, a sizable barge makes its way to and from the island daily through the channel. So keep your head on a swivel when paddling through that section. The best paddling and scenery are in this area, so nobody will fault you if you stay on this side of the island. Alternatively, you can make a complete loop of the island and back to the put-in.

A pair of kayakers put in at Sellwood Riverfront Park.

Ross Island

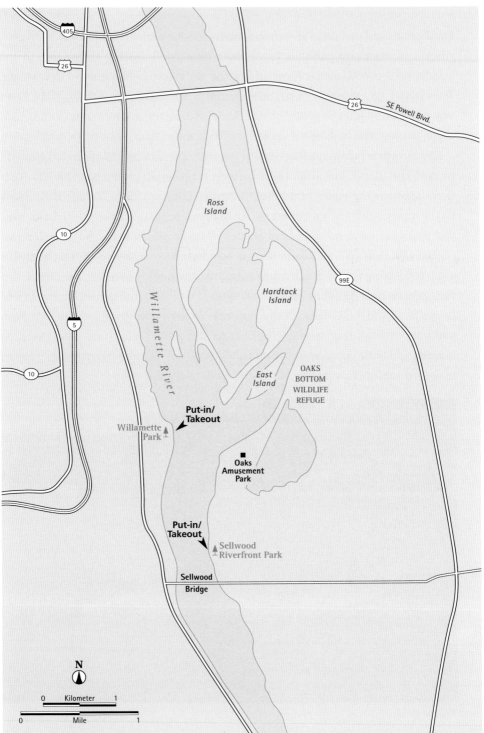

Ross Island

Hardtack Island

Willamette River

East Island

OAKS BOTTOM WILDLIFE REFUGE

Put-in/Takeout

Willamette Park

■ **Oaks Amusement Park**

Put-in/Takeout

Sellwood Riverfront Park

Sellwood Bridge

SE Powell Blvd.

N

0   Kilometer   1

0   Mile   1

A number of different organizations have their hands on Ross Island in one form or another. The island is the site of an extensive urban restoration project, and you are welcome to explore its beaches as long as you stay below the "ordinary high water mark."

If you go before work, you can go flatwater paddling on a mighty river, around an island that pretty much guarantees a handful of nonstandard wildlife sightings, and still make it to the office on time. If you go after work, you can get the same nature rush and be home before dinner.

Local Information

Post-paddle food and drink: Jade Bistro & Patisserie, 7912 SE 13th Ave., or Sellwood Public House, 8132 SE 13th Ave., on the east side; Buffalo Gap Saloon & Eatery, 6835 SW Mac-Adam Ave., or McMenamins Fulton Pub & Brewery, 0618 SW Nebraska St., on the west side

Adventure 31: Willamette Narrows

South of Portland, the Narrows of the Willamette River are basalt rock formations carved out by the Missoula Floods at the end of the last ice age. Now the Narrows present a rock-based obstacle course of channels and islands that morph dramatically with the water level.

County: Clackamas

Put-in: Willamette Park Bernert Landing and dock in West Linn

Takeout: Same as put-in

Distance: Typically 1 to 5 miles

Float time: Self-dependent

Difficulty rating: Easy in low water; intermediate to advanced in high water

Rapids: Can present some whitecaps of consequence depending on water level, particularly in high water

Waterway type: Wide and deep river; several narrow channels and eddies through the Narrows

Current: Minimal in low water; fast current in high water

River gradient: N/A

River gauge: N/A

Land status: City park

Nearest town: Portland

Boats used: Canoe or kayak

Season: Year-round

Fees and permits: None

Schedule: N/A

Maps: *Oregon Road & Recreation Atlas*: Page 106 H4–5

Getting there: From Portland, take I-5 South to I-205 North. Take exit 6 and make a right onto 10th Street. Turn right onto Willamette Falls Drive and then left on 12th Street to where it dead-ends at Volpp Street. Make a left onto Volpp and then a right into the boat launch parking area. GPS: N45° 20.341' / W122° 38.961'

THE PADDLE

The Narrows can run the gamut from a tranquil, easy paddle up to a rollicking thrill ride—and everything in between. The channels and islands that form the Narrows grow and shrink with the water level of the Willamette; and as you might imagine, currents, eddies, potential lines, and everything else change commensurately. You never know exactly what you're going to get until you're in it. So if you're a beginning paddler, start with low water levels, familiarize yourself, and work up to the higher water. The islands in this area are under the management of The Nature Conservancy and Oregon Metro, the elected government for the Portland metropolitan area. They are open to the public, but please be mindful of the habitat.

From the put-in, head south, which is upriver on this part of the Willamette. On your right you'll immediately paddle past where the Tualatin River joins the Willamette. How you explore the Narrows is completely a matter of personal choice. One good low-water route is to paddle along the west side of

Still water on the east side of the Willamette Narrows.

Willamette Narrows

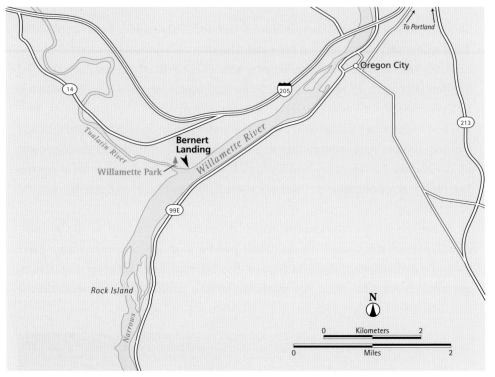

the Willamette and look for the first island of the Narrows, straight ahead. You might want to avoid the channel on the east side of the river, as it eventually dead-ends.

Paddle just to the left, or east side, of the first island, paddling toward Rock Island, the large landmass in the middle of the river. Stay left, or on the east side, of Rock Island, making your way through a channel. Paddle under a set of power lines and continue toward the end of Rock Island, which will appear as a small passage on the right, depending on water level. You can paddle through here, but I recommend veering left and then upriver, exploring the islands and channels of the Narrows.

If you continue paddling upriver, you'll eventually spit out of the Narrows. Paddle to the right and begin heading downriver, with Rock Island and its numerous satellite islands to the east. Paddle over to the west side of the river and hug the shore, making your way into another channel formed by the first island you encountered at the beginning of the paddle. There's more exploring to be had here. As the channel tightens, cliffs rise on the left and small passages between mini-islands open on the right. Once past the island, continue paddling downriver to the put-in at Willamette Park, just past the mouth of the Tualatin River on the left.

During fast or high water, paddling against the current through some of the channels is not possible. Consider paddling upriver against the west bank and returning downriver through the channels.

Local Information

Post-paddle food and drink: J. Willy's Public House & Eatery, 1717 Willamette Falls Dr., West Linn

Adventure 32: Scappoose Bay

Not far north of Portland, Scappoose Bay is a labyrinth of explorable channels teeming with wildlife. Herons and ospreys reside in abundance, and there are myriad options for flatwater paddling. The bay can be ideal for beginners or family outings, but there are enough scenery and exploration opportunities to hold any paddler's interest.

County: Columbia

Put-in: Boat launch area at the Scappoose Bay Marina

Takeout: Same as put-in

Distance: Self-dependent

Float time: Self-dependent

Difficulty rating: Easy

Rapids: None

Waterway type: Bay

Current: Low

River gradient: N/A

River gauge: N/A

Land status: Public

Nearest town: Portland

Boats used: Canoe or kayak

Season: Spring and winter

Fees and permits: Launch fee

Schedule: N/A

Maps: *Oregon Road & Recreation Atlas:* Page 33 H10–11

Getting there: From Portland, take US 30 West for 25 miles to Bennett Road. Make a right onto Bennett and then a quick left onto Old Portland Road. Turn right onto Bayport Marina Lane. There is a staging/launch area and a separate parking area. GPS: N45° 49.661' / W122° 50.276'

THE PADDLE

Fingering off from the Multnomah Channel, Scappoose Bay is a protected waterway that is home to myriad explorable wetlands and waterways. Some of the channels can be a bit dicey or inaccessible in low water, so be choosy with regards to low-water route selection.

Heading into the channel at Scappoose Bay

From the put-in, some of the best exploring is located directly across the bay and to the south. A number of waterways and channels bend around in every direction here, including an access to small but scenic Bryce Lake if water levels are high enough. Herons and ospreys are numerous here, as is other wildlife. If you're paddling in mid- to late summer, your roaming options may be limited. If water is low, try paddling north. You'll eventually meet up with the Multnomah Channel and eventually the Columbia River if you go far enough. Heading in this direction will provide a lot of open-water paddling as well as views of Mount

The Scappoose Bay Paddling Center, run by Portland's iconic outfitter Next Adventure, is located right at the launch area. They provide rentals, classes, tours, and pretty much anything else you might need for an outing on the bay. Contact Scappoose Bay Paddling Center at (503) 397-2161, or visit nextadventure.net/scappoose-bay-paddling-center.html.

Scappoose Bay

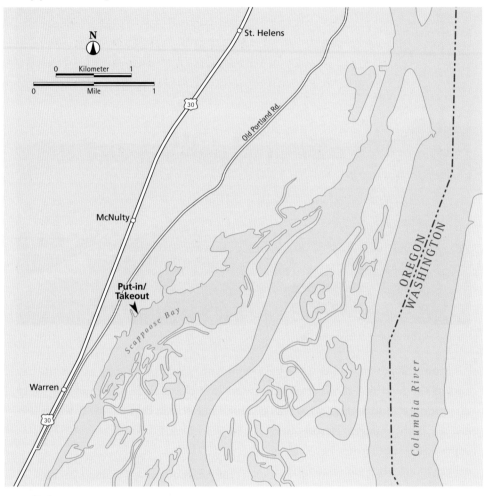

St. Helens. Watch out for boat traffic, however. Paddle out as far as you see fit and return the way you came.

Local Information

Post-paddle food and drink: In St. Helens, check out SunShine Pizza, 2124 Columbia Blvd., or Klondike Restaurant & Bar, 71 Cowlitz St.

Adventure 33: Timothy Lake

A pristine lake in the middle of the forest with a Cascade peak in the background is a scene that's never going to disappoint. Sitting on the south side of Mount Hood, Timothy Lake, formed as a result of the Timothy Lake Dam, is a great place to paddle. There's just over 2 square miles of water to explore and several fetching lunch spots around the lake.

County: Clackamas

Put-in: At the Oak Fork, Gone Creek, or Hood View Campground launch area

Takeout: Same as put-in

Distance: Self-dependent

Float time: Self-dependent

Difficulty rating: Easy to moderate

Rapids: None; potentially choppy when windy

Waterway type: Lake

Current: None

River gradient: N/A

River gauge: N/A

Land status: National forest

Nearest town: Government Camp

Boats used: Canoe or kayak

Season: Late spring through early fall

Fees and permits: Northwest Forest Pass or day-use fee

Schedule: N/A

Maps: *Oregon Road & Recreation Atlas:* Page 49 C11

Getting there: From Portland, take I-84 East to exit 16 and follow signs for US 26 East. Drive around Mount Hood and through Government Camp, making a right onto Oregon Skyline Road. Following signs for Timothy Lake, make a right onto FR 57 and put in from the Oak Fork (GPS: N45° 6.957' / W121° 46.293'), Gone Creek (GPS: N45° 6.796' / W121° 46.543'), or Hood View Campground (GPS: N45° 6.482' / W121° 47.483') launch area.

THE PADDLE

Timothy Lake is about a 50-mile drive from Portland. At an elevation of 3,200 feet, the area can hold onto snow for a while. But once summer is in full swing,

A kayaker paddles her way toward a better view of Mount Hood.

the lake becomes quite popular. An 11-mile loop trail circumnavigates the lake, and there are a number of campgrounds as well as camping spots on the lake's north end that are only accessible via boat or hiking trail. More than 250 designated camping spots line the lake, making it an excellent place for kayak camping. Depth is never an issue, as Timothy Lake averages 45 feet deep, maxing out around 80 feet. The water is quite clear and quite cold. Boats are limited to 10 miles an hour, so wake isn't much of an issue either.

From your chosen put-in, it's entirely a choose-your-own-adventure kind of affair. There are, however, some highpoints you'll want to check out. From the recommended put-ins, Mount Hood will already be in view. If you make your way clockwise around the lake, views will open up and close off from time to time. Passing by the Timothy Lake Dam in the southwest corner of the lake, continue paddling toward the jutting prominence

Timothy Lake is the headwaters of the Oak Grove Fork of the Clackamas River. This fork joins up with the Clackamas River a short ways downstream from the put-in for a fantastic whitewater paddle (see the Clackamas River adventure). This is a great area.

Timothy Lake

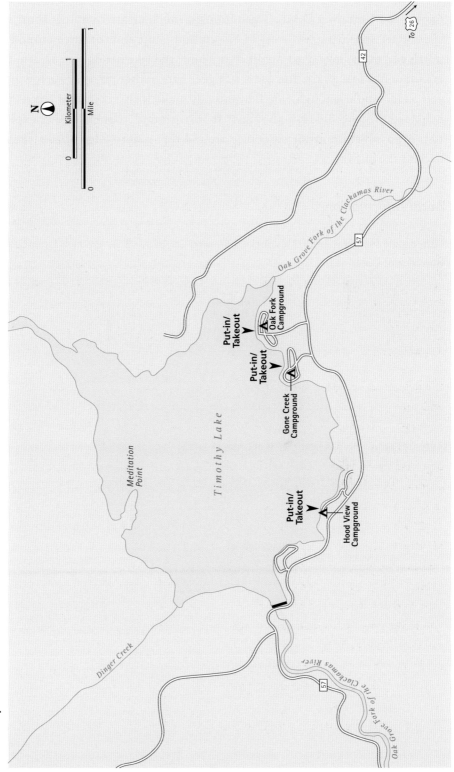

known as Meditation Point. If you brought lunch or are camping, some nice spots start appearing just west of Meditation Point and continue around the north end of the lake. Past Meditation Point, the lake bends into an arm that is a lot of fun to explore. The waterway goes back rather far, ever narrowing. If you paddle in far enough, you'll eventually make it to a couple of creeks that help feed the lake. This is a good spot to turn around, though further exploration is possible. Continue clockwise around the eastern edge of the lake and back to the put-in.

Local Information

Post-paddle food and drink: Mount Hood Brewing Co., 87304 E Government Camp Loop, Government Camp

Adventure 34: Clackamas River

Named for a native tribe that once called the area home, the Clackamas River offers some of the best whitewater rafting in Oregon. It also happens to be the closest whitewater to the city of Portland. Flowing roughly 80 miles from its headwaters near Olallie Butte, the Clackamas carves a path through the Cascade Mountains before joining the Willamette River south of Portland. In 1988, 47 miles of the river came under protection of the Wild and Scenic Rivers Act. Twenty-seven of those miles have been deemed recreational. Depending on time of year and put-in location, you can get the full river experience, ranging from lazy river to Class IIII+ whitewater. Rafters tend to prefer the section of river between Three Lynx and Memaloose, while kayakers tend to run Fish Creek to Bob's Hole.

County: Clackamas

Put-in: Sandstone Bridge

Takeout: Memaloose takeout

Distance: Self-dependent

Float time: Self-dependent; guided trips in half- and whole-day options

Difficulty rating: Easy to moderate

Rapids: Class I to Class IIII+

Waterway type: River

Current: Moderate

River gradient: Average, 132 feet per minute (fpm); maximum, 160 fpm

River gauge: 250 to 500 cubic feet per second (cfs)

Land status: Public

Nearest town: Estacada / Three Lynx

Boats used: Canoe, kayak, raft

Season: Best in spring and early summer

Fees and permits: None

Schedule: Daylight hours

Maps: *Oregon Road & Recreation Atlas:* Page 49 C–D9

Getting there: From Estacada, head east on OR 224. If you're setting out by your-self, put in at the Sandstone Bridge near milepost 41 on the Clackamas River Highway (GPS: N45° 07.000' / W122° 04.537') and arrange a shuttle at the Memaloose takeout near milepost 35 (GPS: N45° 11.681' / W122° 12.988').

THE PADDLE

The Clackamas is perhaps Portland's favorite river for recreation, and it's no wonder. It passes through narrow gorges with steep canyon walls, flows incredibly clear, and visits stately stands of old-growth forest along with a number of campgrounds and feeder streams. A popular hiking trail parallels the river, as does OR 224. The highway is a useful tool for potential paddlers—it allows you to scout the rapids you'll be running later without causing much of a traffic distraction.

From Sandstone Bridge the first major rapid is Powerhouse (III+). During high-water season this rapid possesses some strong currents that can be trouble if you're not paying attention. By late summer you'll want to put in below this rapid.

After Powerhouse things relax a little with a series of smaller rapids coupled with excellent canyon views. Next up, the Narrows is an easy rapid through a scenic gorge. Roaring River (III) is the next rapid of consequence. At

Rapids in a forested canyon segment of the Clackamas River.

Clackamas River

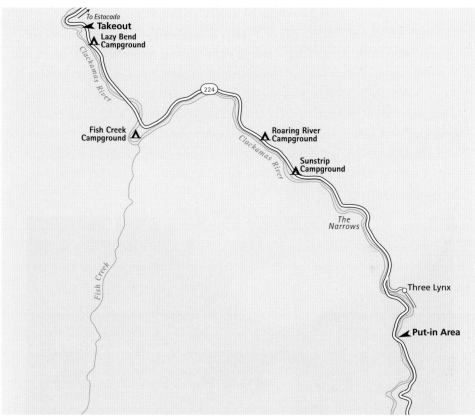

high-water flows there is a large hole at the bottom of the rapid; at low water it gets rocky.

Hole in the Wall (IIII), about 1 mile downriver from Roaring River, is a potentially dicey rapid with an eddy on the left that has a penchant for getting rafters stuck. This is one you'll want to pay extra attention to. After another 1.5 miles you'll encounter Fish Creek. This is a good place to take out (or potentially start) if you are in a time crunch. There is a boat ramp here, and this is the most common put-in for kayakers looking for a short run. Most of the classic play spots on the Clackamas are located on the 3-mile section of river below Fish Creek. After two smaller sets of rapids, Fish Creek and Armstrong, the river opens up just before a larger rapid at Carter Falls (IIII-). Watch for a hole in the center here.

WILD AND SCENIC RIVERS

The Wild and Scenic Rivers Act of 1968 was created by Congress to preserve certain rivers with outstanding natural, cultural, and recreational values in a free-flowing condition for the enjoyment of present and future generations. As of December 2014, less than one-quarter of 1 percent of the nation's rivers were protected by the act. Of all of Oregon's miles of rivers, only 2 percent are protected, but that is still more than any other state! If you live in Portland, you are day-trip driving distance from three whitewater paddles on Wild and Scenic Rivers: the Clackamas and Deschutes in Oregon and the White Salmon in Washington.

The Rogue River in southern Oregon is just one of almost sixty Wild and Scenic Rivers in the state.

Below Carter Falls you'll tangle with two smaller rapids, Slingshot and Rock and Roll, before getting to the Toilet Bowl (III+). This one is a notorious raft flipper during higher flows, so be forewarned. Shortly thereafter, Bob's Hole is an enticing Class III- that marks the end of Class III and above rapids. Although most kayakers take out up the rocks at Bob's, the river below Bob's Hole contains some entertaining Class II rapids before the takeout at Memaloose.

Local Information

Post-paddle food and drink: Fearless Brewing Company, 326 S Broadway, Estacada

Recommended outfitter: Blue Sky Rafting, (503) 630-3163; e-mail: Info@blueskyrafting .com

Adventure 35: White Salmon River

The White Salmon River runs 44 miles from the slopes of Washington's Mount Adams to the Columbia River. In 1986 the lower White Salmon River was designated Wild and Scenic. In 2005 the upper river was awarded the designation. The two segments total 27.7 miles, of which 6.7 miles are "Wild" and 22.3 miles are "Scenic." Of the three rivers described in this book that offer whitewater, the White Salmon offers the best bang for the buck. Because the river is spring fed, it maintains good water levels year-round. The water is clean and cold, and the river pinches through narrow chasms and gorges that produce fast-moving water and a wide range of rapid classes. The raftable length of the river has something for everyone, but the section between BZ Corner and Husum Falls is crammed with Class III up to Class V whitewater. If water levels are right, you can take a run at Husum Falls. The 10-foot falls is labeled a Class V rapid and is the tallest commercially raftable waterfall in the United States. This is some of the best whitewater in the state of Washington, and definitely the best near Portland.

County: Skamania

Put-in: BZ Corner day-use area

Takeout: Husum, Northwestern Park, or a parking pullout at the mouth of the Columbia River

Distance: Self-dependent; typically 5 or 8 miles

Float time: Self-dependent; typically 2 to 3 hours

Difficulty rating: Intermediate

Rapids: Class II to Class V

Waterway type: River

Current: Low to strong

River gradient: Average 45 fpm

River gauge: 500 to 2,000 cfs

Land status: Public

Nearest town: Stevenson, Trout Lake, Washington

Boats used: Raft or kayak

Season: Spring through fall

Fees and permits: Self-permit at BZ Corner

Schedule: Daylight hours

Opposite: Husum Falls

Maps: *DeLorme: Washington Atlas & Gazetteer*: Page 101 A8

Getting there: From Stevenson, take WA 14 East and make a left onto WA 141 North in Underwood. Following signs, stay on WA 141 North for about 10 miles into the town of BZ Corner and the day-use launch site area, on the right. GPS: N45° 51.104' / W121° 30.590'

You can take out at Husum (GPS: N45° 48.012' / W 121° 29.158'), Northwestern Park (GPS: N45° 46.779' / W121° 30.982'), or a parking pullout at the mouth of the Columbia River (GPS: N45° 43.773' / W121° 31.429').

THE PADDLE

The White Salmon River was named by the Lewis and Clark Expedition when they observed the river almost overflowing with salmon that had turned white after spawning. The river traces a collapsed lava tube, and in addition to providing excellent whitewater, the stunningly beautiful river is home to a substantial list of flora and fauna, including a returning salmon population. That's thanks in large part to the 2011 removal of the Condit Dam, once used for hydroelectricity. The dam's removal allowed the river to run unimpeded for the first time in nearly a century, enabling salmon to return to their historic spawning grounds.

There isn't much of a warm-up from the put-in at BZ Corner. The action begins almost immediately with the Class IV Top Drop. Shortly thereafter you pass beneath the Glenwood Road bridge and into an amazing stretch of whitewater. The next 2 miles or so are almost nonstop, with a series of Class III rapids: Grasshopper, Siwash, Corkscrew, and Waterspout. After a bit of a breather, the aptly named Class III+ Stairstep drops over a series of ledges.

Enjoy the scenery for the next mile or so of relatively calm water, because after a little more than 4 miles of total paddling, you'll come upon Husum Falls. You should know what you're doing and scout ahead before trying to run the 10-foot Class V rapid. On approach there's a signed takeout on the right if this is the end of your journey. If you're continuing, there's a portage trail on the left side of the river. There tends to be a lot of traffic in this area and, more than likely, spectators on the bridge that crosses the river at the falls. On the best of days, there will be plenty of kayakers and rafters who are unable to stay upright through the falls. Fortunately, the penalty for failure here isn't brutal, and there's ample opportunity to recover post-falls.

White Salmon River

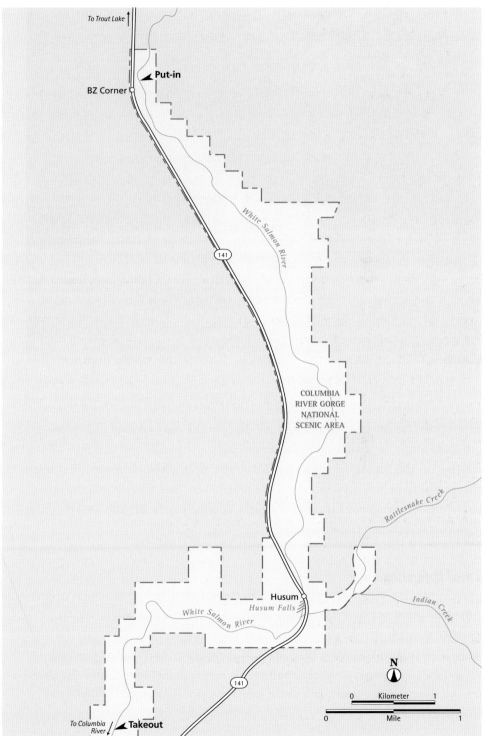

To Trout Lake

Put-in

BZ Corner

141

White Salmon River

COLUMBIA
RIVER GORGE
NATIONAL
SCENIC AREA

Rattlesnake Creek

Husum
Husum Falls

White Salmon River

Indian Creek

141

N

To Columbia
River   Takeout

0   Kilometer   1

0   Mile   1

The clear, cold waters of the White Salmon River

After Husum a series of cooldown Class II and Class III rapids will keep you entertained for the last few miles of paddling to the next takeout at Northwestern Park. Since the removal of the Condit Dam, the paddle can continue all the way out to the mouth of the Columbia River. Be advised, however, that even though the river has more or less settled into its new line, there is still the potential of encountering hazards and/or debris. Carefully scouting this area or going with an outfitter is recommended.

Local Information

Post-paddle food and drink: Everybody's Brewing, 151 E Jewett Blvd., White Salmon, Washington

Recommended outfitter: Zoller's Outdoor Odysseys, (509) 493-2641, www.zooraft.com. While there are a number of reputable outfitters operating on the White Salmon River, I've been on numerous trips downriver with the Zollers and can't recommend the family-run business enough.

Adventure 36: Deschutes River

The Deschutes River is yet another Oregon waterway protected by the Wild and Scenic Rivers Act. Located on the other side of the Cascade Mountains, the landscape is decidedly different from most of the other adventures described in this book. It's about a 2-hour drive from Portland to Maupin, the recommended put-in for this paddle. The Lower Deschutes affords a great variety of easy paddling mixed with bursts of Class II–III whitewater through deep, river-carved gorges. While the drive to the Deschutes River is a bit of a jaunt from Portland, it's well worth the trek. This is a good one to turn into an overnight or multiday excursion if you're so inclined.

County: Wasco

Put-in: Maupin City Park small craft launch area

Takeout: Sandy Beach takeout

Distance: 6.5 miles

Float time: Self-dependent; typically 2–3 hours

Difficulty rating: Easy

Rapids: Class II to Class III

Waterway type: River

Current: Low to moderate

River gradient: 12 fpm average

River gauge: 3,000 to 8,000 cfs

Land status: BLM, public, and tribal lands

Nearest town: Maupin

Boats used: Raft or kayak

Season: Spring and winter

Fees and permits: Watercraft fee at put-in; permit fee at Sandy Beach takeout

Schedule: Daylight hours

Maps: *Oregon Road & Recreation Atlas*: Page 51 B7

Getting there: From Portland, take I-84 East for 84 miles to exit 87. Take OR 197 South for 38 miles to the town of Maupin. Drive through town and then, just after a bridge crossing of the Deschutes River, hang a hard left onto Bakeoven Road. The entrance to Maupin City Park is on the left, just after the Imperial River Company. Park at the small craft launch area. Put-in GPS: N45° 10.422' / W121° 4.456'; takeout GPS: N45° 14.419' / W121° 2.939'

THE PADDLE

The Deschutes is a long river. From its source at Little Lava Lake in central Oregon, the Deschutes flows 252 miles to the Columbia River. It is central Oregon's mecca for outdoor river-based pursuits, specifically paddling and fishing. Perhaps adding to the allure, a lot of human history has transpired along the Deschutes. For thousands of years native tribes used the waterway to access the Columbia River. Sharp eyes can spot petroglyphs on canyon walls in the section of river described in this adventure. The French named the river *Riviere des Chutes*, or River of the Falls, for Celilo Falls on the Columbia, near the mouth of the Deschutes. Because of damming, Celilo Falls has been underwater for quite some time, but it was one of the most sacred gathering spots for native tribes for at least 11,000 years, as much as 14,000 years by some estimates. Until it was submerged in 1957, it was the oldest continuously inhabited settlement in Oregon and perhaps North America. The Lewis and Clark Expedition noted the river, and it was also encountered by those traveling along the Oregon Trail.

Surf City is the first rapid of consequence from the put-in. The Class II+ rapid begins after a long stretch of flat water and can usually be run right up the

A quiet moment on the Lower Deschutes

THE DESCHUTES RAILROAD WAR

Given its geography, constructing a railroad through Deschutes Canyon was not going to be a picnic for anyone. In fact, engineer Henry Abbot didn't think it was in the cards at all, stating, "Nature seems to have guaranteed it forever to the wandering savage and the lonely seeker after the wild and sublime." And this was a guy who worked on the Panama Canal.

That didn't stop two competing railroad companies from giving it a go, however. By midsummer 1909 crews from the Oregon Trunk and the Des Chutes Railroad began building two parallel railroads up Deschutes Canyon on opposite sides of the river. The combination of unsavory conditions and competitive natures eventually produced friction between the two camps. Dynamiting, induced landslides, sabotage, brawls, and even the occasional gunfight led to casualties.

By the end of 1909, both sides had suffered enough and agreed to use the Oregon Trunk line from North Junction to South Junction and from Metolius to Bend. Both railroads would also use the 24 miles of Des Chutes Railroad track from South Junction to Metolius. With a truce in place, the railroad building continued without incident. Remains of all this railroad madness can be seen during the Deschutes River paddle.

middle. The long wave train offers numerous spots to surf and is understandably popular with kayakers.

Just around the corner, the Class III+ Oak Springs rapid is next. Named for the springs that emerge from the canyon in this area, this is one of the highlights of the run. If you're doing this paddle without benefit of a guide service, you'll want to scout this rapid from the road ahead of time—there's a pretty significant drop involved. The best run is on the far left of the channel on the right. Continuing, the White River rapid may be a slight step down in excitement level from Oak Springs, but it's still a bona fide Class III rapid, located near the mouth of the White River. Yet another Wild and Scenic River, it is said that the White River is one of only a handful of rivers that allow you to see the source (the White River Glacier on Mount Hood) and the outlet at the same time. Unfortunately, you'll be negotiating a rapid about this time and probably too busy to notice, but it's nice information to have.

Deschutes River

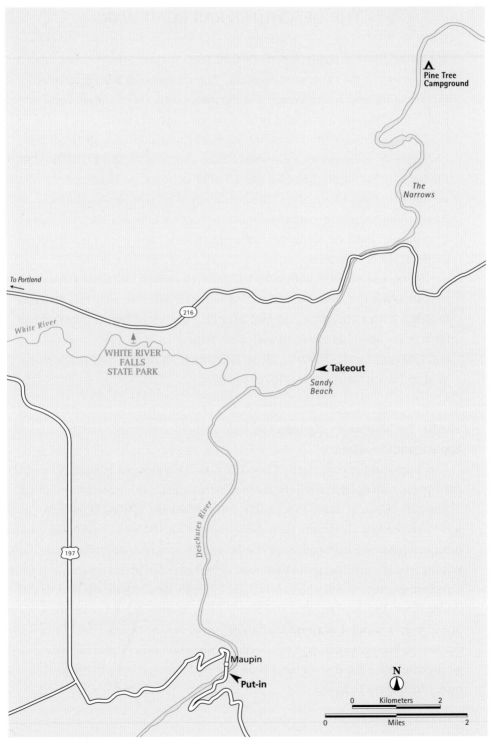

Pine Tree
Campground

The
Narrows

To Portland

216

White River

WHITE RIVER
FALLS
STATE PARK

◄ Takeout

Sandy
Beach

Deschutes River

197

Maupin

Put-in

N

0   Kilometers   2

0   Miles   2

White River Falls

After White River you'll enjoy a few minutes of easy paddling before reaching the Upper Elevator. This Class III cruiser is a swimming rapid. If it's hot out and you're in a raft with others, take a dip. The Lower Elevator is a rolling Class II wave train that signifies the end of the run. If you're with a guide service, this will be the last opportunity to "ride the bull," or sit up on the front of the raft and get wave slapped.

Shortly after the Lower Elevator, look for the Sandy Beach takeout on the right. It's vital that you take out here because Sherars Falls is just downriver. And that's a real day-ender.

If you're a fan of waterfalls, one of Oregon's most spectacular and unlikely cascades is located at White River Falls State Park, not far from Maupin. The two-tiered, 110-foot cascade is jaw-droppingly beautiful and only requires a short but steepish 0.25-mile walk down a dirt path for a complete view of the falls. To get there from the town of Maupin, head north on US 197 for 9.6 miles. Turn right onto OR 216 and drive for 4 more miles to White River Falls State Park. Park at the signed lot near the falls.

OTHER ADVENTURES

With all of the top-tier paddling, hiking, and biking available in the greater Portland area, it's easy to overlook some of the other outdoor activities at your disposal. These aren't exactly afterthoughts, either. If you're into rock climbing, ziplining, or disc golf, you already know that there are some mighty fine places to enjoy those endeavors in our neck of the woods—maybe one of these is new to you. If you're not familiar with or haven't had the opportunity to enjoy these other adventures, maybe now's the time.

The aerial obstacle course at Tree to Tree Adventure Park

Rock Climbing

Rock climbing has a relatively long and storied history in the state of Oregon. In 1983 Alan Watts introduced sport climbing to the United States at Smith Rock. To this day, Smith Rock remains a premier rock climbing destination and a pilgrimage for many. Even though Smith Rock might be a bit too far away to be considered an adventure near Portland, climbers need not worry; there's enough quality climbing here to entertain and challenge enthusiasts of every level. The same volcanic flows that helped form the rest of the region's lauded outdoor recreation are also responsible for the numerous basalt cliffs that are a magnet to climbers. This chapter covers three of the area's premier spots: Broughton Bluffs, Beacon Rock, and the Ozone Wall.

Smith Rock is considered the birthplace of sport climbing in the United States.

Recommended Climbing Shops and Guide Services

Portland Rock Gym (portlandrockgym.com/guiding/) offers private guided climbs from experienced AMGA, SPI guides. Half-day and full-day options are available. Portland Rock Gym also offers introductory rock climbing classes in the gym and at local crags (portlandrockgym.com/learntoclimb/).

Climb Max Mountaineering (climbmaxmountaineering.com). Over twenty-five years of industry experience and a singular focus on climbing make Climb Max Mountaineering the spot for climbing equipment and repairs in Portland.

Next Adventure (nextadventure.net/climbing/). Detecting a theme here? Next Adventure does it all, and they do it all well. That includes everything you need for climbing.

Adventure 37: Broughton Bluffs

Rating: 5.7–5.13

Climb type: Traditional and sport

Land manager: Lewis and Clark State Recreation Site; oregonstateparks.org/index
.cfm?do=parkPage.dsp_parkPage&parkId=116

Fees and permits: None

Maps and guidebooks: *Oregon Road & Recreation Atlas*: Page 107 D9. *Portland
Rock Climbs* and *Northwest Oregon Rock* cover the area.

Getting there: From Portland, take I-84 East to exit 18. Drive south a short distance to the Lewis and Clark State Recreation Site, on your left. From the parking
area, walk south along a gravel path to the base of the bluff. Follow a bootpath
onto the south slope to the Hanging Gardens Wall. The trail to the right quickly
leads to the Red Wall; the left-hand path heads to the base of the Hanging Gardens Wall and on to the North Face.

The Climb

Perhaps the best legitimate climbing within close proximity of downtown Portland, the Broughton Bluffs sit on the eastern shore of the Sandy River near
the mouth of the Columbia River Gorge. One of the area's favorite local crags,
Broughton provides a variety of challenges for nearly every skill set.

Broughton Bluffs offer a little something for everybody on a series of 160-
foot cliffs within the Lewis and Clark State Recreation Site. Broughton is good
year-round but best in summer and fall; with everywhere else around here, it can
be a little wet and slick during the rainy season.

Difficulty ranges from 5.7 to 5.13. The easiest route is the Hobbit Hole (5.7,
traditional) on the Hanging Gardens. Fun and unique, the Hobbit Hole takes off
from the first pitch on Hanging Gardens and worms up through a detached dihedral. This is the toughest spot of the climb, thanks in part to the lack of visibility.
Climb your way through the darkness and into the light. Another favorite, Bad
Omen (5.12b, sport; 1 pitch, 65 feet), ascends the Bat Wall. There are two cruxes
here, and more than one spot that requires a bit of thought and planning. Gorilla
Love Affair (5.10d, sport) on the Jungle Cliff is another classic climb. A technical
ascent that provides a few rests along the way, it's difficult. But it's arguably one
of the most engaging and outright fun climbs the bluffs have to offer.

Bridge Cliff

BORING VOLCANIC FIELD

The Boring Volcanic Field is named for the community of Boring, Oregon, roughly 12 miles southeast of Portland. The area is dotted with low volcanic shields, or monogenetic volcanoes. Rising as high as 650 feet, these buttes were formed during single eruptive events. More than eighty small volcanic vents and associated lava flows dispersed throughout the Portland metropolitan area.

At about 57,000 years old, Beacon Rock is the youngest volcano in the Boring Volcanic Field. Today, all that is left of the cone is the central plug; the rest was scoured away by the Missoula Floods. All existing Boring volcanic centers are extinct, but the Boring Volcanic Field might not be. Since activity started 2.6 million years ago, it is unusual that 50,000 years have passed without an eruption. The probability of an eruption, however, is quite low. In the interim, feel free to explore the buttes. Many exist now as parks with all the trappings, including hiking trails. Some of the more popular include Powell Butte (adventures 10 and 20) and Mount Tabor.

A number of volcanic buttes lie between Portland and Mount Hood.

Broughton Bluffs

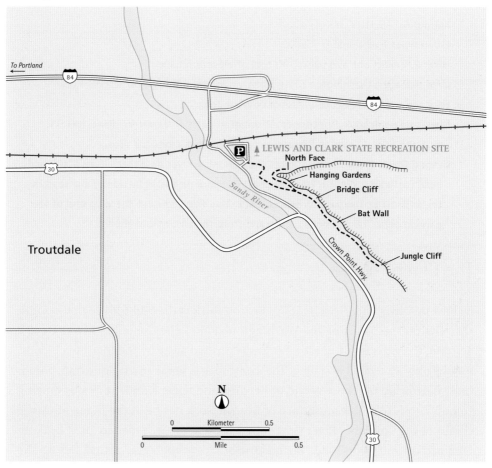

Most of the rock climbs at Broughton have established belay anchors for rappelling without topping out. If you do top out on either the North Face or the Hanging Gardens Wall and prefer a scrambling descent, there is a third-class ridge crest between the cliffs.

Local Information

Post-climb food and drink: Check out Tad's Chicken 'n Dumplins, 1325 E Historic Columbia River Hwy., in Troutdale. Right on the banks of the Sandy River off the Old Historic Highway, it is old-school awesome.

Adventure 38: Beacon Rock

Rating: 5.7–5.11d

Climb type: Traditional

Hike: 2.0 miles out and back; 700 feet of elevation gain

Land manager: Washington State Parks, parks.state.wa.us/474/Beacon-Rock

Fees and permits: Discovery Pass or day-use fee

Maps and guidebooks: *DeLorme: Washington Atlas & Gazetteer:* Page 100 D3.
Portland Rock Climbs and *Northwest Oregon Rock* cover the area.

Getting there: From Portland, cross the Columbia River on either I-5 or I-205 and
head east along WA 14. Near milepost 35, park on the right side of the road in
the pull-off at the base of Beacon Rock. The hike begins at the west end of the
parking area. The climber's path starts from the east end of the lot.

The Climb

Named by Lewis and Clark in 1805, Beacon Rock is the 848-foot-high monolith
that sits on the banks of the Washington side of the Columbia River. Once a
volcano, the exterior of Beacon Rock was washed away by the Missoula Floods,
leaving only an eroded lava plug. The iconic rock is home to a unique trail, potentially harrowing for those afraid of heights, and some excellent climbs ranging
from 5.7 to 5.11d. The south face of Beacon Rock has been the home of classic
climbs in the Columbia River Gorge since it was first ascended in 1954 by John
Ohrenschall and Gene Todd. The northwest face is open year-round, but it's the
south face that has been giving climbers a feel for big wall climbing for decades.

The rock was purchased by Henry Biddle in 1915. Biddle, with the aid of his
donkeys, constructed a unique trail to the summit of Beacon Rock. Consisting of
dizzying hand-railed bridges, ledges, and switchbacks, the trail was completed in
1918. In the 1930s Beacon Rock was almost blown to bits as part of a US Army
Corps of Engineers jetty project. In an attempt to save Henry's labor of love, the
Biddle family offered the rock to the State of Washington in hopes that the area
would become a state park. Washington legislators initially showed no interest,
until Oregon stepped in to accept the gift. This prompted a change of heart in
Washington, and shortly thereafter Beacon Rock State Park was born.

Opposite: Beacon Rock

AREA GEOLOGY

Some serious geological events contributed to the landscape that outdoor enthusiasts currently enjoy in the Portland area. The Columbia River Gorge was formed by a combination of the longest lava flows and largest floods the world has ever known. Between 10 and 15 million years ago, a series of lava flows poured over the landscape, occasionally making it all the way to the Pacific Ocean. Many of the layer cake–looking levels of flow can be seen in various spots along the Gorge.

At the end of the last ice age, the ice dam that kept Lake Missoula in place breached, unleashing a series of floods as high as 800 feet tall, traveling as fast as 80 miles an hour. The floods scoured out the Gorge, creating many of the waterfalls we see today. In addition to a lot of water, the floods brought topsoil from eastern Washington and chunks of granite encased in ice. The granite boulders, known as erratics, can be found all over the Willamette Valley, including on top of buttes. The floodwaters emptied into the valley. As a result, the topsoil is as deep as 0.5 mile in some places, helping contribute to a growing region some call the nation's new breadbasket, and making Portland one of the best places on the continent for farm-to-table cuisine as well as wine.

The Columbia River Gorge, looking westward from the Nick Eaton Ridge

The catwalks leading to the top of Beacon Rock

Henry Biddle's trail to the top of Beacon Rock remains to this day. So in addition to being a great place to climb, there's the added bonus of being able to take one of the more unusual hikes in the Northwest—a 2.0-mile round-trip, 700-foot elevation gain hike, to be precise. To hike to the top, follow the marked hiking trail around the west side of Beacon Rock. The path starts traditionally enough but fairly quickly transitions into catwalks. Pass through a gate (subject to being locked in hazardous conditions) and continue the 1-mile-long trek to the top. The views are inspiring, and they get better with elevation. There are a couple of nice spots at the top for a snack, but not many. Head back the way you came.

For climbers there are a number of epic climbs to be had, starting with the South East Corner (5.7, traditional; 5 pitches, 600 feet). The most popular climb on the rock, this is a great option for newer climbers getting their toes wet with multi-pitch routes. The Flying Dutchman (5.10b, traditional; 1 pitch, 80 feet) is a straightforward but tough, left-facing dihedral with finger locks and stemming. Windwalker (5.11d, traditional; 1 pitch, 90 feet) requires a face climb on gear to make the ridge and a crux negotiation just before a roof.

Beacon Rock

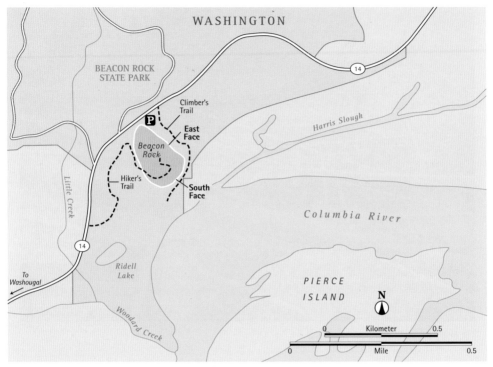

There are some things climbers should keep in mind:

Climbing is limited to the south and northwest faces. The south face is open approximately July 15 to January 31 and is typically closed February 1 to July 14. The seasonal closure helps protect peregrine falcon nesting habitat.

The northwest face is open year-round and is located entirely in the forest, starting at a sign to the right of the water spigot at the parking lot and ending where the hiking trail heads back to meet the wall. This area is posted with signs describing where climbing is off-limits. Also, watch out for poison oak.

Local Information

Post-climb/hike food and drink: Check out the Big River Grill, 192 SW 2nd St., or Walking Man Brewing, 240 SW 1st St., just up the road in Stevenson.

Adventure 39: Ozone Wall

Rating: 5.6–5.12+

Climb type: Traditional and sport

Land manager: Washington State Department of Transportation, wsdot.wa.gov;
  USDA Forest Service, Northwest Region, www.fs.usda.gov/main/r6/home

Fees and permits: None

Maps and guidebooks: *DeLorme Washington Atlas & Gazetteer:* Page 100 D2.

Getting there: From Vancouver, Washington, head east on WA 14. About 0.3 mile
  past Belle Center Road, look for a pullout on the right at milepost 23.75. From
  the paved shoulder, look for a narrow dirt trail that angles down eastward under
  the bluff. The path descends to the initial steep cliff section at the far west end
  of the Ozone Wall.

The Climb

The Ozone Wall is the new crag on the block. And with that newness comes
commensurate interest. But the interest is warranted, and not just because it's

The east end of the Ozone Wall from the trail.

Ozone Wall

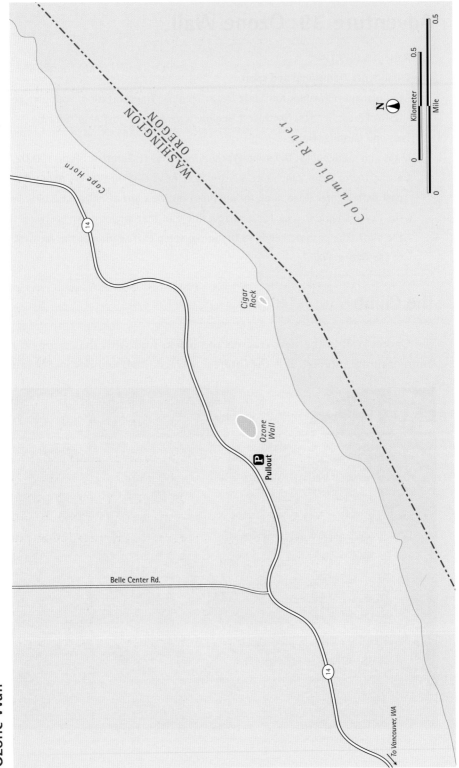

INDOOR CLIMBING

Portlanders are a pretty sturdy lot when it comes to enjoying the outdoors in all seasons. But not all of us are, and even the most hard-core outdoor enthusiasts occasionally opt for warm and dry over cold and wet. Portland has a handful of top-tier climbing gyms that go beyond just keeping you in shape and your skills sharp; they're legitimately enjoyable.

Portland Rock Gym (portlandrockgym.com). As good as it gets, they offer classes, instruction, after-school programs, corporate events, parties, and of course lots of great climbing.

The Circuit (thecircuitgym.com). It's bouldering rather than climbing—slightly different but just as much fun. No equipment, shorter climbs, padded falls.

Planet Granite (planetgranite.com/locations/portland/pdx_faq.php). Indoor climbing with the added benefit of yoga.

a shiny new toy. The Ozone is home to a diverse selection of nearly seventy moderate climbing routes ranging in difficulty from 5.6 to 5.12+.

The Ozone Wall is easily accessed by a short trail hike from WA 14. Bear in mind that all the climbs are lead routes. Most belay anchors are at least 90 feet high, and the cliff is about 120 feet tall.

Be aware that due to the newness of the site, some loose rock still exists. But this issue continues to dissipate as the spot gains popularity. One favorite route, Masterpiece Theatre (5.11c, sport; 95 feet), features a crimp-laden crux with an exhilarating upper arête. High Plains Drifter (5.10c, sport; 75 feet) is benign until the first bolt. From there things get progressively more technical, finishing with a 10c crux near the top.

Local Information

Post-climb food and drink: A couple of great spots are Hearth, 1700 Main St., and Amnesia Brewing, 1834 Main St., in Washougal.

Disc Golf

I f you already enjoy the sport, you don't need me to extol the virtues of disc golf. But since not everybody who picks up this guidebook has had the pleasure of losing a disc into the Ridgecrest Timbers Apartments, allow me to disseminate some basic information.

Disc golf is similar to traditional golf in its basic concept. The primary goal of disc golf is to get a disc into a bucket with the fewest number of throws. There are of course a number of official rules, but at its core, disc golf is easy to understand and easy to start playing. One big difference though—roughly 90 percent of all disc golf courses are free. The startup cost is also low; discs start at around $8 brand-new and can be purchased used for even less. Many courses wind their way through public parks that offer other pre- or post-round activities. Anybody capable of throwing a disc will immediately enjoy the game, while those unable or perhaps unwilling to throw can certainly enjoy the walk. Though the sport may be easy to play, it is difficult to master, giving those looking for a challenge plenty to contend with.

The game can also provide a good amount of "sneaky exercise." For example, during an average round at Pier Park in St. Johns, you can expect to get in roughly 3 miles of cross-country walking. Currently, there are about fifteen courses in the greater Portland area, with more in the works. Disc golf's combination of accessibility and affordability make it a great outdoor activity to add to your repertoire.

Recommended Outfitters

Disc Golf Depot. Seriously, a ton of discs and accessories (http://discgolfdepot.com).

Disc Heroes. This is also a great place to augment your comic book collection (discheroes.net).

Adventure 40: Dabney Disc Golf

One of the Portland area's best courses offers the consummate Northwest disc golf experience: tree-lined holes, open meadows, elevation changes, and water hazards in the form of creeks and ponds. The area's first fully dedicated disc golf course is as challenging as it is beautiful.

Time to complete: 1 to 2 hours

Schedule: Open year-round

Best time to go: Dry weather; summer and early fall

Land manager: Dabney State Recreation Area, oregonstateparks.org/index
.cfm?do=parkPage.dsp_parkPage&parkId=110

Fees and permits: Day-use parking fee

Canine compatibility: Dogs not permitted

Maps: *Oregon Road & Recreation Atlas:* Page 107, D9

Getting there: From Portland, take I-84 East to exit 18. Follow the Historic Columbia River Highway 4 miles to Dabney State Recreation Area. Take the first left to reach the parking lot, which is on the right. Head northeast across the lot and up the road a few yards to the first tee on left, just past the gate.

An open approach at Dabney

Dabney Disc Golf

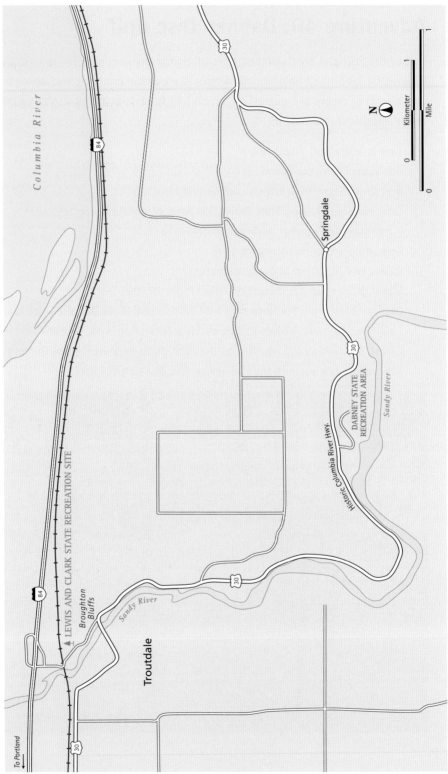

The Course

Dabney is a challenging course that can be a lot of fun if you're a disc golfer with a somewhat developed game. It does have the potential to be frustrating for newcomers to the sport, however. Many of the baskets are hidden from the tee box, there are water hazards, and signage can occasionally be confusing. As with most courses, this will be a tough row to hoe the first time around; but if you're looking for a challenge, the course will become more of a joy with each visit. The wide array of terrain and elevation changes ensures the need for some thoughtful shot making that will also elevate your game.

The course is laid out nicely and will require you to make a number of different shots. In addition, the course features paved tee pads with benches at each one and frequent changes to pin placement. Every hole is different and nuanced in a way that you'll likely use most of the discs you brought.

Aside from the disc golf, this is a scenic little stroll. And that's always been one of the draws of disc golf anyway—it's like a hike with a purpose. Dabney is a beautiful state park. And if you're not a seasoned disc golfer or you're bringing non–disc golfers to the party, the walk through Dabney will keep anyone who enjoys the great outdoors satisfied.

It can be a muddy track, however. If there has been any sort of precipitation in the last 48 hours, you're going to know all about it. And if you're playing during winter or spring, you'd best be wearing waterproof shoes. But you know this. You're living in the Northwest; none of us are made of sugar.

Local Information

Post–golf food and drink: Tad's Chicken 'n Dumplins, 1325 E Historic Columbia River Hwy., Troutdale. It's right around the corner; if you haven't been, you should at least check it out.

Adventure 41: Pier Park Disc Golf

Just after the quaint, Mayberry-esque main drag of St. Johns, Lombard Street gives way to residential development. And just before residential surrenders to industrial, there is an exquisitely designed multiuse park—home to what is perhaps the best in-city disc golf course in Portland.

Time to complete: 1 to 2 hours

Schedule: Open year-round

Best time to go: Dry weather; summer and early fall

Land manager: Pier Park, portlandoregon.gov/parks/finder/index.cfm?property id=513&action=ViewPark

Fees and permits: None

Canine compatibility: Leashed dogs permitted; off-leash dog park, Chimney Park, right next door to Pier Park

Maps: *Oregon Road & Recreation Atlas:* Page 106 C3

Getting there: From downtown Portland, take I-5 to the Lombard exit and head west for 4.7 miles to Bruce Avenue. Turn right onto Bruce Avenue and proceed 0.25 mile to the parking circle. Parking is available along Bruce Avenue, the parking circle at the corner of Bruce Avenue and James Street, and along James Street.

The Course

It wasn't all that long ago that Pier Park was a hub for drug use and A-list crimes and crime-related activities. Then an eighteen-hole disc golf course was installed that visited nearly every corner of the park. In a prime example of the "If you build it, they will come" concept, disc golfers began filtering in from all around the Portland area. The increased foot traffic began to drive out the illicit activity. The safer the park became, the more people visited. And the more people visited, the safer the park became.

From the first tee things are wide open. Don't get used to it though. After the second bucket you head into the trees and stay there. Giant Douglas fir and western red cedar trees greet you on the approach to the third tee. These are the largest you'll encounter, but the tree theme carries through. Some fairways require you to essentially thread the needle through tight, unrelenting forest.

Pier Park Disc Golf

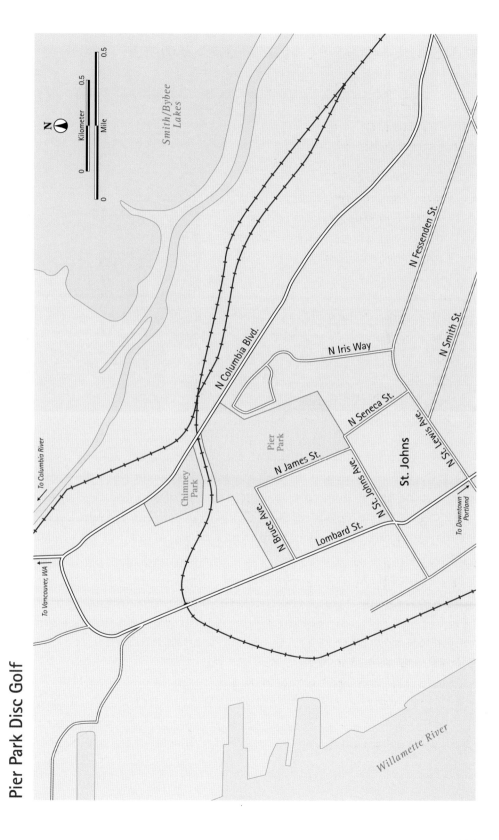

The fourth tee and map at Pier Park

It does get a bit muddy and slick in the wet season, but nothing terrible. In fact, the fall colors around the park are an added benefit when the weather begins to turn. And all those trees that get in the way of your disc traveling more than 25 feet at a time provide excellent shelter from both sun and rain. Pin location changes ensure that par goes from an attainable goal to a near impossibility at times.

Local Information

Post-golf food and drink: Check out Signal Station Pizza, 8302 N Lombard St., or the Fixin' To, 8218 N Lombard St., in St. Johns.

Ziplining

I f you haven't been, ziplining is the act of getting all harnessed up, hitching yourself to a long steel cable via a pulley attached to your waist, whispering a plea of mercy to your deity of choice, and then willfully launching yourself into the abyss. You then go whizzing, sorry, zipping through the air along the cable until you arrive at Point B, where a trained professional prevents you from making too hasty an introduction to Point B. Unclip your pulley from the cable, walk to the next designated jump-off point, and do it all over again. Don't get clammy hands just yet. Ziplining has one of the best "Perceived Risk" to "Actual Risk" ratios out there. In other words, it's safe.

Adventure 42: Tree to Tree Adventure Park

Located on Hagg Lake, the Tree to Tree Adventure Park has an abundance of options. The park not only has a zipline course but also an aerial obstacle course where you can rappel, walk across tight ropes and wobbly bridges, even zipline—all while safely harnessed. Tree to Tree Adventure Park is a great time for anyone, but it's the perfect place for team-building exercises or family outings. The aerial obstacle course comes in three difficulty levels to ensure that everyone is comfortable with the challenge. This place is an absolute joy; plan to be there a while.

Admission to the aerial obstacle course is for 3 hours, with reduced rates for kids 10 and under. Ziplining tours are available. Check out their website at tree2tree adventurepark.com.

Getting there: From Portland, take US 26 West to exit 57. Turn left and follow NW Glencoe Road for 1.3 miles. Turn right onto NW Zion Church road and drive 2 miles. Continue straight onto NW Cornelius Schefflin Road for 1.6 miles. At the traffic circle, take the first exit onto NW Verboort Road and continue 0.4 mile to another traffic circle. This time take the third exit onto NW Martin Road. Drive 1.9 miles and turn left onto OR 47 South. Drive 5.7 miles and make a right onto SW Scoggins Valley Road. Drive 2.9 miles and stay right to stay on Scoggins Valley Road. After 2.2 more miles, make a right onto SW Nelson Road and follow signs to Tree to Tree Adventure Park.

Local Information

Pre-zip food and drink: If you go early, hit Maggie's Buns, 2007 21st Ave., Forest Grove, for a legendary sugar fix.

Adventure 43: High Life Adventures

If you're headed for the coast or are willing to travel a little farther afield, visit High Life Adventures. Just south of Astoria in the town of Warrenton, the family-owned and -operated zipline park sits on 30 acres, with a 7-acre lake smack dab in the middle—a lake you get to zip across a few times and even potentially touch on one descent. Actually, you can get completely doused on this run if you like.

High Life Adventures sports eight lines that total 1 mile of zipping pleasure. They start you off gradually, but things escalate quickly to zipping over lakes, launching backward from 70 feet above the ground, and racing side by side on the last zip.

For fees and hours, visit highlife-adventures.com.

> Getting there: From Astoria, take US 101 south for 2.8 miles; make a left onto Marlin Avenue. Drive 0.3 mile and turn left onto the US 101 Business Loop. Drive 0.8 mile to High Life Adventures, on the right.

Local Information

Post-zip food and drink: If you're heading back through Astoria, you've got solid food and drink options, including the Bridgewater Bistro, 20 Basin St., Ste. A; Baked Alaska, 1 12th St.; Buoy Beer Company, 1 8th St.; and Fort George Brewery, 1483 Duane St.

A brave guest launches off backward from high above the ground at High Life Adventures.

Adventure Index

About the Author

Adam Sawyer is an outdoor and travel writer, photographer, guide, and published author based out of Portland, Oregon. He wrote as the Portland Hiking Examiner for Examiner.com and authored the biweekly column "Portland Family Outdoors" for Craigmore Creations. In addition to writing online for Travel Oregon, Red Tricycle, and Tillamook Coast, his work has appeared in *Northwest Travel, Portland Monthly, Columbia River Gorge, Cascade Journal*, and *Backpacker* magazines. He was the cohost of the KEEN *HybridLife* radio show for its duration and now serves as a sponsored athlete for the company. He is the author of a number of guidebooks, including *Hiking Waterfalls in Oregon* for FalconGuides. Adam is also a professional guide, leading tours that include the Epicurean Excursion for Portland Walking Tours and the Columbia Gorge Waterfalls & Wine tour for Evergreen Escapes.

HEATHER EGIZIO

American Hiking Society

Because you **hike.**
We're with you
every step of the way

As a national voice for hikers, **American Hiking Society** works every day:

- Building and maintaining hiking trails
- Educating and supporting hikers by providing information and resources
- Supporting hiking and trail organizations nationwide
- Speaking for hikers in the halls of Congress and with federal land managers

Whether you're a casual hiker or a seasoned backpacker, become a member of American Hiking Society and join the national hiking community! You'll enjoy great member benefits and help preserve the nation's hiking trails, so tomorrow's hike is even better than today's. We invite you to join us now!

American Hiking Society